RENOVATE

CHANGING WHO YOU ARE BY LOVING WHERE YOU ARE

LÉONCE B. CRUMP JR.

FOREWORD BY MATT CHANDLER

MULTNOMAH
BOOKS

RENOVATE
PUBLISHED BY MULTNOMAH BOOKS
12265 Oracle Boulevard, Suite 200
Colorado Springs, Colorado 80921

All Scripture quotations, unless otherwise indicated, are taken from the Holy Bible, English Standard Version, copyright © 2001 by Crossway Bibles, a division of Good News Publishers. Used by permission. All rights reserved. Scripture quotations marked (NKJV) are taken from the New King James Version®. Copyright © 1982 by Thomas Nelson Inc. Used by permission. All rights reserved. Scripture quotations marked (NRSV) are taken from the New Revised Standard Version of the Bible, copyright © 1989 by the Division of Christian Education of the National Council of the Churches of Christ in the USA. Used by permission. All rights reserved.

Italics in Scripture quotations reflect the author's added emphasis.

Details in some anecdotes and stories have been changed to protect the identities of the persons involved.

Trade Paperback ISBN 978-1-60142-554-6
eBook ISBN 978-1-60142-555-3

Cover design by Kelly L. Howard

Published in association with the literary agency of the Fedd Agency Inc., PO Box 341973, Austin, Texas, 78734.

Published in the United States by WaterBrook Multnomah, an imprint of the Crown Publishing Group, a division of Penguin Random House LLC, New York.

MULTNOMAH® and its mountain colophon are registered trademarks of Penguin Random House LLC.

Library of Congress Cataloging-in-Publication Data
Names: Crump, Léonce B.
Title: Renovate : changing who you are by loving where you are / Léonce B. Crump Jr.
Description: First Edition. | Colorado Springs, Colorado : Multnomah Books, 2016. |
    Includes bibliographical references.
Identifiers: LCCN 2015036163| ISBN 9781601425546 | ISBN 9781601425553
    (electronic)
Subjects: LCSH: Communities—Religious aspects—Christianity. | City missions. | Cities
    and towns—Religious aspects—Christianity. | Religion and geography.
Classification: LCC BV4517.5 .C78 2016 | DDC 248.4—dc23 LC record available at
    http://lccn.loc.gov/2015036163

Printed in the United States of America
2016—First Edition

10 9 8 7 6 5 4 3 2 1

Praise for
Renovate

"Like me, Léonce Crump lives in a racially divided city. Churches in cities like that need help. Help has come in *Renovate*. It's a groundbreaking book to help the church move past racial and socioeconomic divides in order to bring the gospel of Jesus to every person."

> —DR. DARRIN PATRICK, lead pastor of The Journey church in St. Louis and vice president of Acts 29, a global church planting network

"If you find yourself asking questions like 'Why am I here?' or 'What is my purpose?' or 'Will my life count for anything?,' then look no further, this book is for you. Deep, theologically sound, thought provoking, yet delightfully readable and persuasively practical, *Renovate* will change the way you see yourself and the place, the literal place, where you live."

> —MICHAEL FLETCHER, senior pastor of Manna Church and leader, mPact Churches

"In our highly mobile world, we tend to think of where we live as just another stop along the way or, if we are lucky, the final stop on a lifelong journey to find the place that 'fits' us best. Léonce Crump challenges us to consider another paradigm, one that sees the community we live in and minister to as a place to which we've been sent with a calling—a calling to bring God's agenda of redemption to every fabric of life. And when we do, it will change everything, not only about where we live but also who we are."

> —LARRY OSBORNE, author and pastor of North Coast Church in Vista, California

"*Renovate* is a timely disruption in a culture where our attraction to 'progress' can undermine our values and sense of community. With sound theology and urban sensibilities, Pastor Léonce calls into question our tendency to remain disconnected for mobility's sake.

Readers will be inspired to view their current surroundings with new eyes, seeing a call for discipleship and renewal where they once saw only dead ends and dilapidation."

—JUSTIN E. GIBONEY, founder of Crucifix and Politics

"Léonce's voice is what our culture has been missing for a long time. This book demonstrates his unique ability to take very high and complex things and bring them to the street level. This book is a must have."

—PROPAGANDA, Humble Beast Records

"*Renovate* is all about reclaiming a sense of place and a sense of putting down roots, and creating a 360-degree connectedness to the people and experiences within that place. I truly believe the human heart has a deep longing for that place called home both here in this life and in the life to come. Do yourself a favor. Read *Renovate* and reclaim your sense of place."

—LINDA STANLEY, vice president and team leader
at Leadership Network

"With the creative genius of a theologian, the heart of a pastor, the tools of a sociologist, and the attitude of an activist, Léonce Crump has given the church a gift with *Renovate*! He's a master storyteller; he paints a picture of cultural renewal through gospel that will inspire you. Warning: he drops gospel bombs on culture idols. Don't be scared, though . . ."

—DERWIN GRAY, lead pastor at Transformation Church
and author of *The High Definition Leader: Building
Multiethnic Churches in a Multiethnic World*

"Léonce Crump has penned an important work grounded in theological, historical, and current social context. *Renovate* invites us to embrace communities beyond mere sentiment, platitude, or missional project. Indeed, authentic engagement of both neighbor and neighborhood is no longer optional but biblical; not only nice but necessary to advancing a credible gospel witness in an increasingly diverse and secular society."

—DR. MARK DEYMAZ, pastor of Mosaic Church of Central Arkansas and author of *re:MIX, Transitioning Your Church to Living Color*

"In a world where limitless mobility encourages many to constantly pursue the most advantageous option, Crump offers refreshing insight to a theology of place. His ministry in Atlanta and conviction to stay there sheds light on the much-needed conviction of permanent presence. *Renovate* appeals to all ranges of the lived experience, especially in today's society."

—STEPHEN UM, senior minister of Citylife Presbyterian Church of Boston and author of *Why Cities Matter*

"There's a great deal of banter about changing the world. I'm guilty myself as I've also written a book about it. But Léonce Crump is onto something refreshing in *Renovate*. He reminds us of the significant, beautiful, and necessary calling of being faithful, steadfast, prayerful, and present right where we are. In other words, if you want to change the world, begin in your homes and families, pour into young people, get to know your neighbors, and seek the peace of your city."

—EUGENE CHO, senior pastor at Quest Church, founder of One Day's Wages, and author of *Overrated: Are We More in Love with the Idea of Changing the World Than Actually Changing the World?*

"Léonce's new book is provoking yet winsome, smart yet accessible, and loaded with potential breakthroughs. While leading a multicultural movement has given me a platform to teach on the subject for years, I now realize I have much to learn still."

—RYAN KWON, lead pastor of Resonate Church

"Jesus teaches that the central paradigm of the Christian life is to love God with all your heart, soul, mind, and strength, and to love your neighbor as yourself. Léonce Crump's *Renovate* provides a masterful framework for what Jesus's teaching on love looks like across the boundaries of race and class for the twenty-first century. American Protestantism has needed a book like this for the last fifty years."

—ANTHONY B. BRADLEY, PhD, associate professor of
religious studies at the King's College in New York City

"Reading *Renovate* leaves you inspired and challenged to be engaged in the important work of shaping the culture through the gospel. Far too often we regulate Christianity to a Sunday-only encounter, while Crump invites us to join God's work on a daily basis and across the spectrums of life. This is truly a long-overdue call to the people of God to respond to the culture now. It is our time!"

—BRYAN CARTER, senior pastor at Concord Church

"Léonce Crump is a friend and fellow pastor. That also makes him a fellow traveler in our callings to be Christians, husbands, fathers, and pastors. Good fellow travelers teach you to walk the land with sure-footedness and deep-rootedness. They help you see the place you're in, the people you're around, and the possibilities for both. If you want to be better rooted where God has placed you with the people in your family and neighborhood, travel with Léonce in *Renovate*. These pages just might renovate your view of life and how you live it."

—THABITI M. ANYABWILE, pastor of Anacostia River Church

"Few leaders have the theological depth and cultural awareness to speak into the direction of believers in today's world. Not only does Léonce write with the insights of a sociologist; he draws them from personal experience. His writing isn't 'theory for'; it's tried and true testimony."

—LECRAE MOORE, Grammy Award–winning music artist

"Léonce is such a special gift to the church, and a needed one. I'm thankful for his leadership, teaching, and example!"

—JEFFERSON BETHKE, author of *It's Not What You Think*

I dedicate this to my queen, Breanna. Without you, Renovation Church, Renovate the book, my entire ministerial life would not exist. Aside from God, you are the hero of the story. Everyone needs to know it. Thank you for loving me with your whole heart. Thank you for always believing in me. Thank you for never wavering in your trust of Jesus.

Go to the people. Live with them. Learn from them. Love them.
Start with what they know. Build with what they have.
But with the best leaders, when the work is done,
the task accomplished, the people will say
"We have done this ourselves."

—Lao Tzu

Contents

Foreword

Jesus is the King. He is the King over every earthly power and over every spiritual power. He is the one true sovereign to whom all will give an account. He and He alone can extend eternal grace and eternal judgment. Paul tells us "all things were created *through* him and *for* him." Jesus is our loving shepherd and our friend. Jesus has promised to never leave us or forsake us. He will not orphan us. Jesus also sends us out to "make disciples of all nations," teaching them to observe all He commanded. It is knowing that Jesus is King, that He loves us, and that He sends us out that should inform and drive the Christian life. This is where I found *Renovate* to be so helpful. The balance and synergy between these three truths as written by Léonce Crump should be helpful for all Christians regardless of their context.

To be fair, *Renovate* is written with a specific context in view. That context is Atlanta, Georgia. You will see in these pages Léonce's love for this city. He is aware of its history, sociological makeup, and current realities. He hasn't turned his eyes from its brokenness and wickedness, or from the complexities of the urban context. He does write as a man provoked like Paul was in Athens. If you don't find yourself in an urban center or anywhere near Atlanta, there is still plenty to learn from the book in your hands. I pray that more Christians would pay close attention to where they live and minister, and would develop what Léonce calls a theology of place. There are some reasons this hasn't taken place. In my opinion, *Renovate* is spot on about sentness needing to be established among all Christians and not just those who feel called to vocational ministry. I couldn't help but smile as Léonce told stories and dreamed of ordinary church members feeling called into difficult neighborhoods and doing ministry for the long term in a given place. I also was reminded in a new and fresh way that Christians should think of their jobs in a specific way driven more by loving God and neighbor than it should ever be about making money or finding purpose in life.

Léonce will write quite a bit about transculturalism and the ethnic complexities that exist not just in Atlanta but where any sinful men and women dwell near each other. If you are an Anglo brother or sister, some of what he writes might rub you the wrong way and you may be tempted to disregard some of it. My experience with these types of conversations is that the posture of the Christian should be humility with a desire to understand. Your experience probably doesn't walk in step with Léonce's. But it would be a good thing to seek to understand how his experiences and losses have shaped him and how he sees the world around him today.

I have been friends with Léonce for quite a few years now, and I'm glad that the Lord sovereignly crossed our paths. I am eager to see what God accomplishes through his passion and unique gifting. I pray that the Spirit of God would shape, form, and renovate your heart toward Himself and your neighbor. Enjoy reading.

—MATT CHANDLER, pastor of The Village Church
and president of Acts 29 church planting network

Acknowledgments

There are no great men; just great teams that make incredible sacrifices so that the one whom they trust to lead them can get the credit. This is an indisputable fact, and one I feel especially as I consider what it has taken to produce this project. Sure, I wrote it, but it was the elders, leaders, and particularly the staff and community at Renovation Church who inspired it. They not only strive to live out these principles, but they are the test subjects who willingly allow me to try just about anything within reason to see our beautiful Atlanta more readily reflect God's glorious city to come. For this book, they let me step away from the day-to-day grind of leading to write about leading, and for that I am forever grateful. Ralph, Ethan, Copper, Pamela, Dawn, John, Vivian, Samuel, Justin, Leonard, Brian, John S., and Eric, thank you. I love my team. I love our church. I love Atlanta. Without all three, I'm just a man with a dream . . .

Additionally, thank you to my editor, John Blase. You kept me in the fight all the way to the finish line.

Introduction

Do you want your life, the lives of your family and friends, and the life of your community to reflect the glory of God? If your answer is no, then return this book immediately and try to get your money back. I'm not sure you can, but you should try, because you've obviously made a mistake. I'm sorry for your confusion, but these things happen, right? But if your answer is yes, even if you don't know what all that positive answer means or looks like, then I believe you've picked up the right book. And if the timing in your life is right, if your heart and mind are open enough to hear and wrestle with the things I want to share with you, then a powerful equation is in play.

the right words + the right time = CHANGE

That's right. Change. As in honest-to-goodness change. The study of family systems has shown us that when a person changes, the entire family dynamic changes. That truth applies here too. So while we long for change in our communities and neighborhoods and churches and families, it is vital to remember that those changes begin on a very personal level, with each and every one of us. That's what we want, isn't it? For things to be different? We want things to change. *We* want to change. And not just for the sake of change, but for the better. For the good.

THE PROBLEM

I have learned that defining the problem at the outset is always wise. I'll elaborate on the problem and also the answer in the pages and chapters that follow, but for now allow me to simply name them. The obstacle standing in the way of our lives and our communities reflecting the glory of God is transience— defined by Random House Webster's as "1. not lasting, enduring, or permanent; transitory. 2. lasting only a short time; existing briefly; temporary." The world we live in is one of almost limitless mobility. We can, physically and mentally, be almost anywhere in the world at any moment in time. This is truly an incredible time to be alive. But with all our advances in technology, I'm afraid something has been lost. Because of our now limitless mobility, the great majority of us have lost a sense of place that was inherent to previous generations. Sociologist Richard Florida writes,

> First the railroad revolutionized trade and transport as
> never before. Then the telephone made everyone feel

connected and closer. The automobile was invented, then the airplane, and then the World Wide Web. . . . All of these technologies have carried the promise of a boundless world. They would free us from geography, allowing us to move out of the crowded cities and into lives of our own bucolic choosing. Forget the past, when cities and civilizations were confined to fertile soil, natural ports, or raw materials. In today's high-tech world, we are free to live wherever we want. Place, according to this increasingly popular view, is irrelevant.[1]

It seems that, at least from the perspective of most, having a sense of place is antithetical to the postmodern buffet of limitless options and unfettered mobility. In other words, wherever I am right now is the most important place in the world. And wherever I will be next will replace it. But this has not always been the case. Prior to the many technological advances we enjoy, people were unable to move much farther than the place their families settled. Because of an inability to be as transient as we are now, there was a sense of responsibility and ownership, not only for the family unit, but—in the absolute broadest terms—for the very space the family occupied. The community was "ours," and the contribution of each person mattered to the whole.

Today, however, we are free to move from place to place, enjoying the offerings and benefitting from each place's resources. But we rarely stay long enough to invest in its sustainability.

Richard Florida agrees: "We owe it to ourselves to think about the relationship between place and our economic future, as well as our personal happiness, in a more systematic—if different—way. . . . Maybe this seems so obvious that people overlook it. Finding the right place is as important as—if not more important than—finding the right job or partner."[2]

I believe he is on to something. For our own good we must recapture a sense of place. What Professor Florida misses, though, is why it matters. Here's what I mean. If my sense of place is only rooted in my personal happiness or economic future, then my sense of place is as fragile as my emotional state or the sense of stability and personal gain I derive from being economically, relationally, or even creatively secure. Experience tells us that all of these vacillate wildly, and with them so does our sense of place. The bottom line is this: if I am only connected to a community to the extent that it can sustain me, we have a parasitic relationship, and I will siphon its resources without regard to its well-being. In an impersonal sense, it affects the culture of the community. In a personal sense, it affects the people.

THE SOLUTION

There is another view though, one that takes into account the greater good and ultimately the glory of God. This is in complete contrast to transience; it is permanence or staying put. This view places value on people and the places they inhabit.

This view sees worth and meaning in the perspective we take in participating in the life of a community. This view pushes us to see ourselves as sent and not simply existing.

This book is about fleshing out this solution of permanence and developing a theology of place. At the same time, this thread of sentness runs through everything that is said here. They are dependent on one another; you simply cannot have one without the other. I'm not asking you to believe that fully at this early point, but I am asking you to consider it.

CONSIDER TIM AND BECKY

Consider my friends Tim and Becky, owners of Bearings Bike Shop. In 2008, around the same time my family and I moved to Atlanta, they moved from their suburban home into a downtown Atlanta neighborhood. Adair Park is a historic neighborhood in southwest Atlanta, one that has been left behind by the sweeping wave of gentrification. When sharing his story with me, Tim told me something that, judging by the incredible work they do there, I would have never guessed. He said, "We moved here looking for a cheap house on a wide street in the city. We had no desire to do anything but fix up our home and live our life." But soon after moving there, they began to notice the state of their community. In their own words: "As we began renovating our house, we would watch local gangs gather and fight in the neighborhood park. It became apparent that the park was virtually unusable by families. Violence, drugs, prostitution, and crime dominated [our] neighborhood to the point where small children couldn't play on the playground."

Then something incredible happened. They had a sort of awakening. They felt a stirring in their hearts like nothing they had ever experienced before, and in that moment they had a choice. Would they view this place as one to now flee, because it did not offer them the life of promise and personal happiness that so many other places would, or would they determine that the issues plaguing this small community were now *their* issues?

The Bearings Bike Shop's existence is living proof of the choice they made. When they realized they were not just selfishly or purposelessly existing in their neighborhood, everything changed. And though they had not grasped it when they first decided to move, what was happening had now become abundantly clear: God had sent them to Adair Park for the express purpose of being present so they could see the problems pervasive in their community, and, through seeing and experiencing them, develop a deep and rich sense of place.

By God's grace they have invested their lives toward a solution. For five years the Bearings Bike Shop has been an intersection between them and the children of Adair Park. Through their efforts, many of the gang fights have ceased, the children's education levels have risen, children in the neighborhood are taking responsibility for their home by picking up trash and reporting crime, and the adults—those who've moved in from other suburban areas and those who've been there all of their lives—have taken notice. One revolutionary idea, seeing past themselves for the sake of the community, has helped to create a sense of ownership and place for nearly all their neighbors.

What is so gripping about Tim and Becky's story is that they didn't start out with the idea of turning the world upside down. In fact, they started out very much where most of us are: looking for the best opportunity to advance their own cause, to serve their own ends, and to make a life for themselves. But in a moment, everything changed. In a moment, they began to discover why they are where they are. They were *sent*.

AND CONSIDER ME

In April 1963, Dr. Martin Luther King Jr. penned his famous "Letter from Birmingham Jail." Some fellow clergymen had been critical of his presence in Birmingham, calling his activities unwise and untimely. I've had the privilege of viewing some of Dr. King's original notes, scribbled across various pieces of paper—it was a surreal experience for me. Although the letter eloquently lays out several reasons for his presence there, the fundamental reason is summed up in this one thought: "I am in Birmingham because injustice is here. . . . Injustice anywhere is a threat to justice everywhere."[3] Presence itself—in the face of injustice—was a ministry worth his freedom.

My name is Léonce B. Crump Jr., and I am a pastor in the beautiful, broken heart of downtown Atlanta, Georgia. If you want to know why I am here, I would echo Dr. King's words: because injustice is here.

Atlanta is well known for its trade, arts, creativity, and commerce. Some have even described it as "the New York of the South." Even William Tecumseh Sherman, whose army burned Atlanta to the ground, ensuring Lincoln's reelection and ending Georgia's contribution to the Confederate war effort, upon returning to Atlanta several years later, said, in an interview with Clark Howell of the *Atlanta Constitution:* "When I got to Atlanta, what was left of the Confederacy could be roughly compared to your hand. Atlanta was the palm, and by destroying it I spared myself much further fighting. But remember, the same reason which caused me to destroy Atlanta will make it a great city in the future."[4]

Sherman was correct. Atlanta is a great city. But while Atlanta is truly great on one level, on another level my city is clearly crumbling. Consider this: a recent undercover study found more than seventy-two hundred Georgia men sought to buy sex with a child in a one-month period. This is why Atlanta is ranked in the top five cities in America for sex trafficking. There are also more than twenty thousand homeless people in the city on any given day. Women and children make up 70 percent of that number. Fatherlessness, joblessness, poor educational institutions, drug addiction, violence, and orphaned children are just a few of the host of reasons why the heart of Atlanta is shattered. These and others could be summed up by the word *injustice.* And injustice anywhere is a threat to justice everywhere.

That's why I came to Atlanta. And through much trial and difficulty, it's why I've remained. That's why I'm here.

And like Tim and Becky, I, too, was *sent*.

WHAT ABOUT YOU?

One of my hopes is that this book causes you to stand in your community and ask yourself that same question: *Why am I here?* Perhaps, like me, it's because you have a clear view of some injustice that must be overturned. Perhaps it's simply a desire to do *good* in a world that is filled with unequal measures of lasting beauty and visible brokenness. I can assure you, though, there is a reason. You are not there by happenstance. You are there to be a part of God's solution, to meet the need around you. Whether you're aware of the need that surrounds you is another matter. But if you're not, then maybe I can remind you of some biblical truths, share some flesh-and-blood stories, and ask some hard but ultimately answerable questions about what is known as the "ministry of presence." Without these truths and stories and questions, you'll have no context for asking yourself that important question or for pushing yourself to see what lies beneath the accepted narrative of your city or town or place.

And as we'll see, context is everything.

One last word before we begin. The subtitle to this book is *Changing Who You Are by Loving Where You Are.* As you consider and ask questions here, I hope the answers you find are disruptive. I hope the answers you find will cause you to wrestle with some long-held ideas. Ultimately I hope those answers stretch your eyes and mind and heart to the breaking point and beyond, for only to the extent that we ourselves are broken can the love of God sweep in and fill us with a desperate love for the people who surround us and the towns and cities in which we live. Until that happens, we are only noisy and clanging (1 Corinthians 13). Truly, without love we are nothing.

One

Why Are We Here?

Directions are instructions given to explain how.
Direction is a vision offered to explain why.

—Simon Sinek

This book is essentially a renovation project, and as with any such project, it is essential to start with the foundation. Is it sound? Does it need repair in any way? Bypassing the foundation only leads to headache later, so that's where we're going to begin—the foundation. Answering the question "Why are we here?" is our foundation. Discovering God's true purposes for the world He created and our role in it is our foundation. Upon this foundation we will build every other idea presented and hopefully build a holy confidence in you that empowers you to believe that what you are doing, right where you are, right now, matters. There will be some lofty proposals that may disturb what you've always felt to be true, and I certainly won't be able to cover every potential objection exhaustively. My hope, though, is that as you grapple with the possibility that our most common understanding of the phrase "Jesus came to save the world" may be truncated or misguided is that you would do so by first running to the Scriptures and nowhere else to determine whether what is being written here is true or whether I've simply lost my mind. So are you ready? Really ready? Okay then, here we go.

Heaven is not our ultimate hope. Yes, you read that correctly. To take heaven as our ultimate hope, believing that in the end God will simply wipe away the world and start over, has far-reaching effects. Our belief may subconsciously stunt the way we live life and do ministry. Even the difficulty many have with investing long-term in a place, to see a ministry effort through to its end, is connected to our view of what God will do with this world. If you believe our ultimate hope is in heaven, I must ask, what if you're wrong?

FOR GOD SO LOVED *THIS* WORLD

Jesus came to save the world—what an incredibly pregnant phrase, a phrase familiar to most every follower of Jesus. Jesus came not to condemn the world, nor judge the world, but *to save* the world. He says as much throughout the Gospels. He says it with force in His emotion-filled soliloquy at the end of John's narrative, in chapter 12.

> I have come into the world as light, so that whoever
> believes in me may not remain in darkness. If anyone

hears my words and does not keep them, I do not judge him; for I did not come to judge the world but *to save the world*. (verses 46–47)

This phrase captures the thrust of His intentions. It is reflective of God's desires described amid many illustrative statements at the close of His public ministry, and we must consider it with new eyes if we are ever to understand what it means to be fully present in a place, as opposed to transient, and what it means to do ministry in this world, the only world we have.

So I ask a simple but complex question:

How is it that you view this world?

I ask this first because it is fundamental to our discussion. How we view God's world matters with respect to how we treat God's world and how we see ourselves in it. I ask, second, because for centuries we've been taught there is a dichotomy between the sacred and the secular, between that which is of the world and that which is not. This is a sort of Christianized Gnosticism that treats this material world as inherently bad and our being in Christ as purely spiritual, which in turn leaves us completely detached from this world. The unfortunate consequence of this perspective is that many of us have been taught, and therefore believe, that we are pitted against the world as enemies—and if not enemies, then neutral participants—rather than postured toward this world as what I call "redemptive agents." On a more serious front, this has led to an escapism mentality when it comes to the world; namely, we are separate from it and therefore must survive it until we are relieved.

A SILLY GOSPEL

In sillier forms this mentality has led to Christianized interpretations of otherwise normal activities. What, for instance, is *Christian* aerobics or, more controversially, *Christian* hip-hop? The church has created an entire subculture rooted in this sacred/secular divide, which has more to do with separating us from the world than it does with God's intentions for the world. I realize there is nuance here, but in our fear of being too *of* this world, we are all too often not really *in* it either, but merely *on* it, taking up space. Songs and sermons have been written to remand us to the idea that this world is not our home. In one sense, this is true. This world, as it is, is not our home. But have we, in much of our understanding, taken this and created a false dichotomy? According to Scripture it certainly seems we have, and knowing this should make us ask some penetrating questions, such as "Why would we live detached from what Jesus came to save?" and "Why would we believe to be inherently evil (the world) what God once called very good?" In good conscience and right submission to God's Word, we can't. The world is not inherently evil; it wasn't created that way. It has been infected with a disease called sin. This infection was initiated by satanic lies and ratified by the covenant-breaking actions of the first family. The world was made good, and God so loves His world, why would He abandon it?

Here's one way to conceptualize this idea, particularly if you are married or desire to be. Imagine your spouse is suddenly infected with a disease, though it is their own fault that they are infected. They wandered into a quarantined area for no good reason other than they wanted to, and they have now contracted a life-threatening illness. Would you revile them or seek to redeem them? Would you desire to heal them or have them die? Would you desire to save them or see them destroyed? Unless you lack an ounce of humanity, we both know the answer to those questions. How much more, then, would God, in His infinite and unalterable perfection and love, long to keep His covenant with creation, eradicate the disease of sin, and restore His creative work? God wants to win the world, not destroy it! God's ultimate desire is to restore the world, not wipe it away. This world is not an evil place needing to be escaped from, but an infected place needing to be renewed, to be restored, to be renovated. Make no mistake, these are competing worldviews. The escapist route is best captured by that word I've mentioned a few times already—*transience*—which may be the ministry problem, if not life problem, of our time. The renovating route evokes words like *perseverance, faithfulness, long-suffering, staying put.*

This is the narrative of the Scriptures—God's continued revelation of His covenant relationship with humanity and creation. What we have, then, in Jesus repeatedly declaring that He came to save the world rather than rid God of it is so rich with meaning that we must embrace it, not only for how it affects our view of our future, but for how it impacts the way we live now, where we live now, and what we do day-to-day in our present reality.

BACKWARD UNDERSTANDING

You've probably heard some variation of the quote, "Life can only be understood backwards; but it must be lived forwards." The source is the Danish philosopher Søren Kierkegaard, and his point was that clarity for our lives forward lies in looking to the past. That's how it works here, as we look back to the very beginning. The Scriptures open with a dramatic tone. "In the beginning, God created the heavens and the earth. The earth was without form and void, and darkness was over the face of the deep. And the Spirit of God was hovering over the face of the waters" (Genesis 1:1–2). If you are a Christian, then you have likely read these words, perhaps many times. You have more than likely taken them as a simple account of what took place when the world was made. But what if I told you that these few words, and what follows for the next two chapters, are revealing for us far more than just a simple narrative of God's creating everything from nothing? What if I told you that what is being revealed to us in actuality is God covenantally binding Himself not only to humanity but to the full breadth of His creation? But what does that mean, exactly?

A covenant, in brief, was a typical way of describing a relationship bound by promises and obligations. The word *covenant* can be found 286 times in the Old Testament and is a common feature of the ancient world, particularly in Middle Eastern cultures. When Moses writes that God created the heavens and the earth, what he is shaping immediately for the reader is that God was establishing a covenantal relationship with His world. What comes next is familiar to most. After these substantial opening words, God begins to create, and with nearly everything He creates, He immediately calls it good. The Scriptures record an almost rhythmic continuation of just that—He creates, He calls it good. In this we see the declaration of God's unchanging covenant with the totality of His creation. Everything He made, He sustains. And everything He made is meant to obey Him. Everything is bound covenantally to God (see Psalm 145).

> All things, plants, animals, and persons are appointed to be covenant servants, to obey God's law, and be instruments . . . of His gracious purpose.
> —John Frame, *The Doctrine of the Knowledge of God*

While that quote is true, there is a nuance when it comes to "persons." Among all the things God created, humanity is different. Human beings are the one creature created, called, and empowered to bear God's image within the rest of His creation.

Then God said, "Let us make man in our image, after our likeness. And let them have dominion over the fish of the sea and over the birds of the heavens and over the livestock and over all the earth and over every creeping thing that creeps on the earth."

So God created man in his own image,
    in the image of God he created him;
    male and female he created them.

And God blessed them. And God said to them, "Be fruitful and multiply and fill the earth and subdue it, and have dominion over the fish of the sea and over the birds of the heavens and over every living thing that moves on the earth." (Genesis 1:26–28)

Human beings were created to mediate the rule of God to His world. We were given stewardship over everything, trusted with everything. A failure to be faithful to God on our part affects all of creation. We were made accountable to our Creator for His cosmos, His world.

To miss humanity's unique calling in this world would be to miss the very purpose of our being made in God's image.

You see, this understanding only comes by looking back. But this has to leave us wondering, where is the disconnect between what God intended and the world in which we presently exist? In other words, what happened?

So What Happened?

God created all things, and after each successive creative eruption, He deemed it good. After He made humanity, He looked over everything with the admiration of an overjoyed father and deemed it all "very good" (Genesis 1:31). Then a shift occurs. What Moses records following this series of creative events is tragic. Even those unfamiliar with the Bible know the unfortunate end of the first family, and with it the decline of "very good" into disorder and decay.

The Fall. This phrase has come to be the common nomenclature used to describe the events of Genesis 3, a familiar but often diminished incident in history. Though the phrasing grabs our attention, it is far from adequate in describing the utter violation of God's goodness that subsequently brought fracture and discord into God's creation. It is inadequate in describing the devastating infection unleashed on creation that followed Adam and Eve's terrible decision.

The full account of humanity's creation is unpacked in Genesis 2. After God created the man, He gave him a job, to work and keep his new, perfect home. This was a beautiful beginning. We don't have a time line of this period. We don't know how long it lasted or how often God engaged with Adam, but what we read in Genesis 3:8 smacks of familiarity. God is described there as "walking in the garden in the cool of the day." This is written as though it were a common occurrence. God is personal. There is clearly a rich relationship present between the Father and Adam. Within the bounds of this relationship—the relational dynamic of covenant is vitally important—the Father says to Adam, and Adam alone, "You may surely eat of every tree of the garden, but of the tree of the knowledge of good and evil you shall not eat, for in the day that you eat of it you shall surely die" (2:16–17). This was the command. It was clear. Periodically I've wondered to myself, why? Why create a tree that could cause such havoc? But I know I am asking the wrong question. It is not about the tree, but what the tree represented.

> It was not the nature of the tree that made it danger-
> ous . . . but what it stood for: obedience to the word
> of God.
> —Michael D. Williams, *Far as the Curse Is Found*

The tree itself is inconsequential. What's in view is whether this man, created in God's image, endued with God's love, and granted stewardship of God's rule, would trust God's word. It's the exact same struggle all human beings have today. Will we trust God and take Him at His word, or will we trust ourselves and elevate our word over His? Adam's, and subsequently Eve's, answer to that question is all too clear. The ramifications were far-reaching, affecting every aspect of creation and spreading through every generation since them.

Lucifer. The Evil One. Satan. Historically feared, maligned, or made into a playful character, he enters the narrative of Genesis 3 in the form of a serpent, as the voice of reasonable deception. Yes, reasonable deception. He approaches Eve subtly and seemingly without ill intent. Adam is not engaged. The serpent begins his innocent inquiry by simply asking, "Did God actually say, 'You shall not eat of any tree in the garden'?" (verse 1). This is not threatening at first, but is presented as confusion on his part. Perhaps one unfamiliar with the narrative may think he simply misunderstood the command of God. But this was no misunderstanding. This was a coy attempt at dishonoring their Father and inciting rebellion. Eve, having been instructed at some point by Adam as to what God said, responded as if correcting Lucifer's confusion, "We may eat of the fruit of the trees in the garden, but God said, 'You shall not eat of the fruit of the tree that is in the midst of the garden, neither shall you touch it, lest you die'" (verses 2–3).

There is clarity in her response, though minor variations exist in what she says compared to what God commanded Adam. Though it could be perceived that she sees God's instructions as open to human interpretation, at the very least she understands the consequences of rebellion. She knows the ultimate end of choosing wrongly. But the serpent's insistent persuasion doesn't relent at her gentle rebuke. His motives are immediately made clear: "You will not surely die. For God knows that when you eat of it your eyes will be opened, and you will be like God, knowing good and evil" (verses 4–5). The trap was set, the seed sown, rebellion imminent, as the woman suddenly believed a lie. Actually she believed *the* lie, the same one we believe every time we rebel against God's goodness. God must be hiding something from me. God must not have my best interest in mind. God. Is. Not. Good.

THE ALMOST UNDOING OF EVERYTHING

It happens so swiftly that one must read and reread to try to grasp the moment that the woman forsook her relational covenant with God, her calling to steward His rule, her imaging Him in perfection, for some false notion that she could be a better god than God. All the while you must wonder, "What is Adam doing right now?" The original command came to him, did it not? He was made first, was he not? Why would he not, in this moment, step between the serpent and his wife and mediate the mistake that was about to unravel their covenant relationship with God? Perhaps this question is unanswerable, but what we do know is he not only allowed her to be deceived, but he took the deception from her hands, following instead of leading, partaking in death right along with her. "She took of its fruit and ate, and she also gave some to her husband who was with her, and he ate" (Genesis 3:6).

In a single moment, everything God intended is *seemingly* undone. God's relational covenant with humanity is violated. Humanity's stewardship over the whole of creation is distorted. Humanity's capacity to adequately image God is marred. Everything God previously marveled over and called very good immediately began to experience the consequences of Adam and Eve's decision to willfully violate the Word of God and believe the lie of the Evil One.

> Our first parents being left to the freedom of their own will, through the temptation of Satan, transgressed the commandment of God in eating the forbidden fruit; and thereby fell from the estate of innocence wherein they were created.
>
> —Westminster Larger Catechism, Question 21

This was a complete flight from God. Their rebellion invited discord, alienation, and the covenant curse of guilt and death. The narrative then shifts from the conception of rebellion to God's response. God, walking in the garden as He seemingly did with regularity, calls out to Adam, "Where are you?" (verse 9). They were hiding. God is God. His question is not one of location but an almost rhetorical question of spiritual and relational state. He knew what they'd done. They'd never hidden before. Their relationship just experienced a decisive shift. Notice he calls for the man. Why? Because it was to the man that the covenant command was handed down. It was with the man that the covenant relationship was initiated. And ultimately it is the man, God's first son, who is responsible for what has taken place.

DIVINE HEARTBREAK

Upon God's call, the man responds. He is naked and afraid, he tells God. God inquires, "Who told you that you were naked? Have you eaten of the tree of which I commanded you not to eat?" (Genesis 3:11). Again God inquires, not because He lacks the knowledge, but because He is engaging the fracture of their spiritual and emotional state, of their relationship with Him, and of His creation. In response to God's question, they begin blame shifting. It's a common trait that has been handed down to us from the first couple. Adam blames his wife. Eve blames the serpent. God looks on with heartbreak and disgust.

I've often imagined this moment. Painful? Filled with regret? A mix of varying emotions? We often characterize God as distant, as though He doesn't feel. Yet the Scriptures are replete with moments where God expresses deep emotions. We are made in His image after all, however marred it might now be. Where do you think our emotions come from?

God feels:

Anger | Psalm 7:11

Compassion | Lamentations 3:22

Grief | Genesis 6:6

Love | 1 John 4:8

Hate | Proverbs 6:16

Jealousy | Nahum 1:2

Joy | Zephaniah 3:17

Pleasure | Psalm 149:4

Pity | Judges 2:18

I only share this so that you understand that what took place was not some impersonal breaking of God's law but a very personal violation of God's love. We need to have that as the context to understand what happens next.

God, in response to their rebellion, imposes several curses on all involved in this covenant-breaking revolt. His righteous anger was turned on the Evil One first, no doubt leaving the two made in His image to wonder what exactly would be their fate. He curses the serpent to spend forever writhing along the ground, lower than any other created thing. God turns to the woman, promising pain in childbirth and a constant sense of inadequacy that would cause her to long after her husband's role. She would not, unless something dramatically altered the course of human history, ever experience the co-equal but role-designated dominion over the earth that God granted them in Genesis 1:26–28.

God then finally turns to the man, His first made. He rebukes him for submitting to the voice of his wife rather than the command of God. He reminds Adam of His covenant, not only with humanity, but all of creation. God reminds Adam of his role to steward God's rule in the world and the subsequent effects of His rebellion: "Cursed is the ground because of you; in pain you shall eat of it all the days of your life; thorns and thistles it shall bring forth for you; and you shall eat the plants of the field. By the sweat of your face you shall eat bread, till you return to the ground, for out of it you were taken; for you are dust, and to dust you shall return" (Genesis 3:17–19).

You must ask yourself why. Why is the ground itself cursed because of Adam's revolt? When Adam violated his covenant with the Father, everything under his stewardship violated it as well. The consequences, then, extended to every aspect of God's creation. The world would now be experienced as an inhospitable place, human dominion challenged at every turn. Work becomes toilsome instead of joyous. Adam's rebellion shattered the harmony in which God's creation, His entire creation, previously existed. The apostle Paul tells us that the world groans under the weight of sin, though the material universe did not bring that groaning upon itself (Romans 8:20–22). Even the Old Testament prophet Hosea sees the connection between humanity's response to God and the health of the rest of creation.

> There is swearing, lying, murder, stealing, and
>   committing adultery;
>   they break all bounds, and bloodshed follows
>   bloodshed.
> Therefore the land mourns,
>   and all who dwell in it languish,

and also the beasts of the field

and the birds of the heavens,

and even the fish of the sea are taken away. (4:2–3)

The scope of Adam's revolt undeniably includes the entire planet.

GOD DIDN'T RUN

God could have washed His hands, started over, pulled the transient card, walked away, and left things as they were: a sin-sick people inhabiting a sin-sickened world. But God is too good for that. He is too kind. Through one man came death (Romans 5:12), but through another man would come the renovation of all that was broken. Through the second Adam would come life (verse 17).

Found within the words of the curse that God imposed on the serpent is a sliver of *hope*. You could miss it easily if you're not attentive to the character of God or the words being spoken. After God curses the serpent to its lowly existence, He speaks to that which inhabits the serpent: "I will put enmity between you and the woman, and between your offspring and her offspring; he shall bruise your head, and you shall bruise his heel" (Genesis 3:15). God's hostility is directed to the serpent, not the man, not the woman, and not His creation. His war is not against the world He made but against the serpent, against sin and death, against disobedience and rebellion, against anything that would try to threaten His rule. There are essentially two antithetical kingdoms set against each other because of the infection called sin that entered God's world. And God would not lose what is His.

But what, you may wonder, is hopeful in these words? Martin Luther called Genesis 3:15 the *proto-euangelion*—the first gospel. In these words of war, God also declares hope and good news that can only point to the One to come. God announces to the serpent that the woman will be his enemy. She will not follow after him. God will have her as His own, and God will have a people through her as His own. Though they revolted, God will redeem them. This is the extent of the jealously renovating love of God.

In this first gospel, God doesn't stop at announcing this enmity between the woman and the serpent. God is making promises, the greatest of which is that One is coming who will right this grave injustice and alter the course of human history. The He spoken of here is the coming Messiah, Jesus. He will be the One to secure the promises God made. He will be the One who will ultimately crush the head of the serpent and reclaim for the Father all that belongs to Him.

A Grace-Full Transition

This moment of transition from curse to grace is paramount. In opposition to a spirit of transience, God is committing to permanence, ensuring the future of humanity and, with it, all of creation. The narrative ends with two beautiful reflections of God's covenant promise being kept. First, understanding, it seems, what has just taken place in God's war/hope declaration, Adam names his wife. Until this moment she had simply been referred to as "the woman." Now that God has secured for her and her offspring a future free from becoming like the serpent, and promised to form a people for Himself from all people, Adam gives her a name meaning "life" and "mother of all" (verse 20). Second, we see God in a glorious act of grace make the first atoning sacrifice in Scripture, and with the skins of that sacrifice, He covered the nakedness of His two children. He covered their sin in the sense that their knowing their nakedness was a direct result of their rebellion. This is grace. This is hope. This is God's securing what is His and making plain that nothing would stop His intentions. This is the beginning of His great redemption. God did not give up on His world, nor did He give up on His stewards, namely, humanity. God desired a renovation of what once was, and so throughout Genesis we see God seek a renewal of His original covenant: first with Noah, then with Abraham, and then with Israel, and this extends down the generational lines through Jesus to you and me. We are now called, through God's renewed covenant in Christ, to be mediators of His renovation of the entire world. Where Adam and Eve failed, in Christ, we have hope to succeed.

That is why we are here.

What did you find in this chapter to be thought provoking? How would you describe your emotional reaction to the chapter—angered? reassured? challenged? Take a moment and write your responses in the space provided below so you can track your thoughts over the course of this book.

_____

_____

_____

_____

_____

_____

_____

_____

_____

_____

_____

_____

_____

_____

_____

_____

_____

_____

_____

_____

_____

_____

_____

_____

_____

_____

_____

_____

_____

_____

_____

_____

_____

_____

_____

_____

_____

_____

_____

_____

_____

Two

The Way Home

Your kingdom come,
your will be done,
on earth as it is in heaven.

—Jesus

So it is in Jesus, the promised One, that we see so clearly what God is up to. Jesus said that He'd come to save the world—this world, not another. God is not wiping this world away; rather He is in the midst of renovating it, with Jesus spearheading the campaign. In Jesus's life, death, and ultimately His *bodily* resurrection from the dead, we see God's unstoppable goal is nothing less than the total restoration of what He called very good and the total eradication of the disease called sin that has damaged His world.

Jesus is the means, end, and ultimate mediator of God's promise to restore the world He made and to cleanse it of the sickness of sin and all its effects, once and for all.

Jesus is also our way into this story, our Redeemer who purchases our place in this redemption plan. And so when we look back to John's narrative, it all makes sense as to why Jesus would declare that He has come to save the world, and what role we'll ultimately play in its restoration!

> Jesus cried out and said, "Whoever believes in me,
> believes not in me but in him who sent me. And who-
> ever sees me sees him who sent me. I have come into
> the world as light, so that whoever believes in me may
> not remain in darkness. If anyone hears my words and
> does not keep them, I do not judge him; for I did not
> come to judge the world but to save the world. The one
> who rejects me and does not receive my words has a
> judge; the word that I have spoken will judge him on
> the last day." (John 12:44–48)

Jesus came into the world to represent and reflect God in His nature, character, being, and perfection! He came to be a light that revealed not only our and the world's debilitating infection from the disease of sin but to reveal God's intentions toward His world, keeping His covenant and restoring His work. He came to speak the very words of God so that those who obey those words would receive the benefit of being swept up in God's redemptive plan of restoring all things He has made, every aspect of creation. He came so that none could say they did not know what the world was supposed to be like, what God's intentions were for His creation, and what humanity's role was in His work. Jesus came to save the world because God the Father loves the world that He made. God wants to win His world, not destroy it. God wants to heal His world through the purifying blood of Jesus, not wipe it away. God wants to cleanse His world, not replace it. And for some wonderfully strange reason, He wants to uphold His covenant, and He invites us to participate in making our present and future home hospitable and filled with His glory once more.

Okay, but What About Heaven?

Yes, what about it? We know for certain that we will go to heaven when we die. "We are confident, yes, well pleased rather to be absent from the body and to be present with the Lord" (2 Corinthians 5:8, NKJV). We usually leave it at that, giving ourselves a "biblical" ground for escapism. But the Bible doesn't stop there. History won't stop with your or my death, and so neither should we. Getting you to take this turn in understanding has been the primary goal of what you've read so far.

Jesus will return one day to consummate the in-breaking kingdom, but will that bring destruction or cleansing? Renovation or a wrecking ball to the earth? Scripture more readily supports the former: a total renewal of the world. Though an annihilationist view of what will happen upon Jesus's return finds "support" in 2 Peter 3:3–13, this passage, according to theologian Al Wolters, speaks of smelting, not destruction.[5] Purification, not annihilation. The world will not be destroyed upon Jesus's return but will be made as it was intended to be and beyond. There are several places in Scripture that support this so clearly that we'd have to bypass the very words on the page to miss their meaning.

> Jesus said to them, "Truly I tell you, *at the renewal of all things,* when the Son of Man is seated on the throne of his glory, you who have followed me will also sit on twelve thrones, judging the twelve tribes of Israel. And everyone who has left houses or brothers or sisters or father or mother or children or fields, for my name's sake, will receive a hundredfold, and will inherit eternal life. (Matthew 19:28–29, NRSV)

> In this way God fulfilled what he had foretold through all the prophets, that his Messiah would suffer. Repent therefore, and turn to God so that your sins may be wiped out, so that times of refreshing may come from the presence of the Lord, and that he may send the Messiah appointed for you, that is, Jesus, *who must remain in heaven until the time of universal restoration* that God announced long ago through his holy prophets. (Acts 3:18–21, NRSV)

For in him all the fullness of God was pleased to dwell, and *through him God was pleased to reconcile to himself all things,* whether on earth or in heaven, by making peace through the blood of his cross. (Colossians 1:19–20, NRSV)

In fulfillment of his own purpose he gave us birth by the word of truth, *so that we would become a kind of first fruits of his creatures.* (James 1:18, NRSV)

There is no way around this. Scripture does not in any sense present heaven as the hope of the believer, but rather as the place where Jesus presently is until His return. Heaven is the place where Christians who have passed from this life remain until Jesus returns. Heaven is an intermediary place for us (who die in Christ) to enjoy until we return to the place that God made for us in the beginning. God is renovating the entire world because the entire world was drawn into humanity's revolt (Romans 8:19–24). And when it is renovated, it will be our home.

The structure of the biblical drama has matching book covers. . . . It moves from a creation story through a drama of sin and redemption to a consummation in a new and restored creation.
—Michael D. Williams, *Far as the Curse Is Found*

JUST A-PASSIN' THROUGH?

The entire narrative of Scripture, with respect to God's engaging His creation, is one of His coming down—a divine condescension, if you will. God comes down in Genesis, first to commune with His creation, and then in the wake of Adam and Eve's rebellion, to pronounce judgment and hope in one sweeping moment. God comes down in the Gospels in the incarnation of Jesus, as He, fully God and fully man, walks the very world He created. And He dies at the hands of the men and women He came to save. In Revelation, God comes down. The City of God descends, consuming and transforming the world onto which it descends, making it the holy home of God and man together, as we were always intended to be. We won't be going up to God in the end. Rather He will be coming down to us to walk once again with us in the cool of the day.

When the Scripture closes in Revelation 21 and 22, it speaks of material things, not our floating in ethereal space. All things are made new. The "faithless, the polluted, the murderers" (NRSV) are gone. There is a visible city, and it has a name—the New Jerusalem. There are walls and gates, the tree of life, and the river of life. The "nations" are present with God. It is very much a corporeal existence for humanity, one that is a direct reproduction of Jesus's at His resurrection. This form of our world is being renewed, passing away in a sense, but the world itself is not passing away. No. It will remain. And with it—if we don't die before Jesus's return—we will remain.

If we hold an escapist or annihilationist view of God's world and our place in it, then I would say we believe that God is too weak to rid His world of this infection or too fickle to uphold His covenant born at creation.

Simply, our goal is not to get off the planet but to see it renovated. Our goal is to see God heal the infection that affects His world because *this* world is our home.

Jim Reeves, known as Gentleman Jim, made famous the old song "This World Is Not My Home," and it has been sung by the faithful for years.

This world is not my home
I'm just a-passin' through[6]

While those lines can rouse the spirit to look beyond the trials and troubles of today, they do not fully reflect the truth. For that, let me counter with the brilliance of Isaac Watts:

Joy to the earth; the Saviour reigns;
Let men their songs employ;
While fields and floods, rocks, hills and plains
Repeat the sounding joy.

No more let sins and sorrows grow,
Nor thorns infest the ground:
He comes, to make his blessings flow
Far as the curse is found.[7]

What we're talking about here is foundational. In a very real sense, it is a worldview—quite literally the way one thinks about the world. Worldviews are hard to alter, and though I believe you are up for the challenge, I also know we've covered a lot of ground here. Let's pause for a moment and get our bearings. Grapple with these questions as you consider what you've read.

1. Did God not create the world?
2. Did He not call it very good?
3. Did He not rejoice over it?
4. Does He not presently hold all things together?
5. Did He not promise to return?
6. Did Jesus not say that He came to save the world?
7. Why then, would we see this world as a place to be escaped, rather than a place to be redeemed?

Engaging these questions is important, because even if you already believed what's been written, or if you have been swayed in some sense, applying it is another matter. Living in light of our coming reality and our understanding of how this world ends (or doesn't) is a high hurdle. We have to be scripturally reprogrammed to see every day and every act as one that holds redemptive potential.

We have to see that what we do right now and how we do it right now matter. This is the truth that eventually surfaced for me as I moved from simple infatuation with my city to actually having a redemptive perspective and plan to see it more readily reflect the city to come.

This *is* home.

LOVE COMES AFTER INFATUATION

Infatuated. Looking back nearly seven years, that's how I would describe myself when I arrived in Atlanta. I was infatuated with the city and all the potential I saw. I would often just sit and stare at the downtown skyline, mostly at night when it was lit up as though beckoning the world to admire its greatness. The city sometimes seemed to have a life of its own. As I stared, I wondered what mysteries it held in trust. When I wasn't looking at the intricate maze the buildings seem to make with their woven pattern, it was not uncommon for my wife and me to stand atop our building and watch the fireworks over Turner Field after a Braves game. In each of those moments I felt a sense of awe considering what might lie ahead.

To me Atlanta was teeming with art, business, culture, diversity, and creativity, and I was going to be a part of making it better. I had a grand plan for how the church, my church, would be intricately involved in the continued rebirth of intown Atlanta, our place.

There was only one problem. I didn't know anything about what had made Atlanta what it was when I got here. I had no idea why Grant Park seemed to be consuming neighboring

Summerhill, and I didn't know the history of Summerhill itself. I had no idea why the Memorial Corridor seemed to contain only the remnants of what had once been several booming industrial complexes. I had no idea why the pastors and churches in and around our neighborhood did very little to work together to serve the communities they were in.

It would take three failed attempts and false starts of a three-times renamed church plant before I would finally see the writing on the wall. In all of my admiration of the city, I knew little more about it than what demographic studies tell you: who's there, crime rates, school "worthiness," but little else. In other words, I really didn't know anything.

It wasn't until I began asking questions, lots of questions, that things truly came into focus. My daily routine changed dramatically, and the bulk of my time was then invested in coffees, lunches, drinks, and conversations. I determined that I would hear as many stories from native or near-native Atlantans as possible.

> To [know these places] well, to really come to an
> understanding of a specific American geography,
> requires not only time but a kind of local expertise,
> an intimacy with place few of us ever develop. There
> is no way around the former requirement: if you want
> to know you must take the time. It is not in books. A
> specific geographical understanding, however, can be

sought out and borrowed. It resides with men and
women more or less sworn to a place, who abide there,
who have a feel for the soil and history, for the turn of
leaves and night sounds.[8]

I gathered the perspectives of those who'd moved into the
city from the suburbs, most of them children of those who'd
fled the city at their birth or shortly after, looking for better
schools and greener pastures. I gathered the stories of grand-
mothers who feared losing their homes to rising property taxes,
though they'd been living in their homes in some cases for
thirty-plus years. Their understanding of intown neighborhoods, what the interstates had done to cut them off, leaving
several of them in pockets of isolated poverty, and how white
(primarily) and black (secondarily) flight has affected the city
was invaluable.

A Story Is Told in a Thousand Pictures

I gathered the stories of the poor, homeless, and multi-job-
holding single mothers who were striving to make ends meet.
What I heard from their hearts cannot be fully captured in
these few words, but what I can describe, in short, is that they
were people—human beings with hopes, dreams, fears, and
desires. Even if they presently lived on the street, they, too,
longed for a better city. Single mothers longed for a place with
better schools and more opportunities. They desired all the

things every person desires, but they felt almost helpless in attaining them.

Through these stories, which unearthed for me details I'd never considered (such as why Moreland Avenue suddenly changes to Briarcliff Road when it crosses Ponce De Leon Avenue; that is, to disassociate one wealthy area from a more impoverished area), I began to understand where God had sent me. Did you catch that word? *Sent.* I began to understand the complicated task in front of us. I began to see I could not impose my vision on these people, but I had to allow the context to teach me how it would be reached, how Atlanta—and the people who called Atlanta home—would be transformed by the gospel. In a very real sense I had to go to school, to sit in the classroom of my place. And school always involves history lessons.

With that in mind, I need to tell you a short story, a brief history of my city, a little detail and data to substantiate the many anecdotal tales that will form much of the substance of this book. My challenge to you, as you read, is for you to wrestle with another question:

Do I know enough of the history of my place to effectively see it renovated?

Your answer to that question could be the difference between fidelity and transience. No, I take that back. Your answer will be the difference.

PERSPECTIVE FROM THIRTY THOUSAND FEET

I fly quite a bit, probably more than I should, and one of the more interesting sights, with which I remain intrigued, is the image of what could be seen as two rivals. One is Atlanta, rising on the horizon like a great metropolis. Glass skyscrapers gleaming in the sun as though saluting its worthiness to shine down on them. The other is the community of Buckhead, from all appearances as formidable as Atlanta. This scene is almost surreal every time I experience it. The city of Atlanta and the community of Buckhead face each other like rival kingdoms in some medieval tale. Everything from the posture of the buildings to the topography of the land upon which they sit seems to lean with inherent opposition. They look to be pitted against one another.

Perhaps this image would not be so strange if one of these cities was not in actuality a vital part of the other. Perhaps this image would not be so strange if the history of the birth of one of these cities was not commingled with intentional racism, classism, and abandonment of the city of Atlanta.

I don't for a moment imagine you are as interested in history as I am, but every place has a history that has shaped and formed the demographics, the population density or lack thereof, and wealth/resource distribution. Every city has scars, left behind from years of calculated and sometimes cataclysmic decisions. As I share some of the history of my place, I challenge you to start grappling with the history of your own. Your knowledge, even partially, of these scars is paramount to your knowing why you are there, what you can do, and exactly how it is you will apply the principles of renovation and presence.

Simply put, you can't make a plan for people you don't know. Not in a personal sense (your relational connections in a place) or a broader sense (the history of where you are). If you do, you've come to your end before you've even begun. Believe me, I know this *personally*.

I cannot stress enough that for you to truly transform a community, you have to understand how it came to be in the first place. So take a moment. Think about it. How well do you *really* know the place where you are? Can you narrate its story? Can you place names and faces on the ideas and structures that presently govern its existence? Do you know why God needed to send you there? Permit me then to flesh some things out by bringing this discussion to ground level in Atlanta, away from the aerial view that only shows me what has been built, down into the places, faces, and litany of decisions that led to what has been built. To do that I'll have to help you understand, at least in part, the rebirth of Atlanta's rival to the north—Buckhead.

POLITICS, RACE, AND THE UNMAKING OF A CITY

The year 1965 was considered by many to be a banner year for Atlanta. Even Dr. King, at an event in Philadelphia, said, "We're building, as you know, a new South, a greater South. And in a real sense, Atlanta is one of the brightest and most promising spots of that new South."9 But on April 4, 1968, just three years after these generous words, Dr. King was martyred, the full impact of his growing legend never experienced. For more reasons than can be recounted here, his death was not in vain. Dr. King's death would come to mark the closing of one chapter and the beginning of another, not only with respect to the civil rights movement, but with respect to his home, the city of Atlanta. His death would signal a new day when the African American leaders of the city would insist on having a more prominent seat at the table, alongside those who'd long ruled every facet of Atlanta's public life.

By 1969 change was fully in motion. After campaigning tirelessly throughout the year in an African American church almost every Sunday, Maynard Jackson was sworn in as Atlanta's first African American vice mayor in January 1970. His ensuing political career would be a major catalyst to the quickening pace of the shifting racial and economic dynamics in the city of Atlanta. His presence and push for equity would eventually help to undo the facade of polite tolerance under which most Atlantans existed at the time. We'll return to him in a moment, but first you need to understand the landscape upon which his battle would be waged, as it was complicated to say the least.

Atlanta had sprung from the post–World War II era relatively unscathed by the racial tensions experienced in the rest of the southern United States. Described as "a city too busy to hate" by longtime Mayor William Hartsfield (for whom our airport is named), Atlanta had managed to escape the riots and violence associated with the fight for equality, and the rewards were enormous: rapid growth, corporate and individual wealth, the arrival of major league sports, and recognition as the capital city of the South. Unfortunately, the reward was not reaped equally by all. For generations there had been a clear dominance of one group over another. Though "black life" was in some sense allowed to proliferate, there was still an unspoken understanding of place, pace, and role in the shaping of my city.

The white power structure (sociologist Floyd Hunter coined the term) governed nearly every decision that affected Atlanta, from which businesses came into the city, to what political offices were filled, by whom, and who was allowed to develop certain sectors of the city. This group included Robert Woodruff, the head of the Coca-Cola Company who "through cross-ownership and a web of interlocking boards of directors" was well known to have been "the final authority in several other institutions in Atlanta."[10]

This was Atlanta. The city too busy to hate, and simultaneously too segregated to truly love. During those tumultuous banner years of the sixties, nearly every restaurant was still segregated, and only five of Atlanta's hotels freely accepted black guests.

And so we return to Maynard Jackson, who is credited with singularly reshaping the desire for political influence among Atlanta's African American leadership. He first burst onto the scene in an idealistic campaign for senator in 1968, running against Atlanta's infamous segregationist incumbent and former governor Herman Talmadge. What was at first seen as little more than a ruse turned out to be the beginning of a massive change in Atlanta.

Jackson, though he lost the Senate campaign, would not only go on to win the now-obsolete vice mayor role, but he also would be Atlanta's first African American mayor just three years later. To win this office he had to defeat Sam Massell, Atlanta's last (at present) white mayor. Massell's defeat and Jackson's rise caused two things: (1) it assured African Americans that they now had a place at the table and an opportunity to shape the future of the city in which they lived, and (2) it prompted many Anglo Atlantans, who would not passively allow the city to be "taken over," to flee and form new places for themselves. In this transition, Buckhead was reborn.

Too Young to Die

In the winter of 2009 my wife and I attended an open house event in my neighborhood. One of the beautiful turn-of-the-century mini-mansions in Grant Park had just been placed on the market, as its renovations had finally been completed. We went only to take in the scenery; this home was far out of our price range. So were many other homes in my rapidly gentrifying neighborhood. While we were there I engaged in an extended conversation with the owner/rebuilder, and he turned out to be a sixty-five-year-old native of the city. He was an Anglo brother, and he was filled with stories, including a few about his attending worship services at Dr. King's father's church—Ebenezer Baptist Church. With a story that I have tried to fact check repeatedly (to no avail), he shared his understanding of the birth of Buckhead, and its connection to the election of Atlanta's first African American mayor. When I say birth, I don't mean its actual beginnings as a suburb, but rather its birth as a rival to the city from which it sprung. According to my new sage, when Sam Massell lost the election of 1973 to Maynard Jackson, he apparently met with several city business leaders and declared, "Let them [African Americans] have the city. We'll take the money."

Like all oral tales, there is some indication this is truth mixed with memory. And though there have been denials over the years that this conversation ever took place, what has been recorded without dispute are Massell's words, displayed in the headline of a two-page ad in the *Atlanta Constitution* in 1973. In the ad that he took out, he'd written "Atlanta's Too Young to Die."[11] Some might have considered his words the Hail Mary of a losing politician. But the reality was his words reflected the lengths he and many other white business leaders were committed to in order to accelerate the explosion of the northern suburbs and the near-complete abandonment of the city of Atlanta.

COSTLY GROWTH

For nearly fifty years after World War II, Atlanta's economic and population growth skyrocketed, almost entirely in its northern suburbs. The motivation for this shift northward was at first overtly racial, caused by many things including the election of Atlanta's first African American mayor, Maynard Jackson. It eventually became a self-reinforcing trend. Many Anglo Atlantans fled north in ever-increasing numbers, primarily to distance themselves from the city's African Americans, who were then and are even now largely relegated to the southwest part of the city. The factors surrounding this flight were many, but none were so volatile as school desegregation.

In the same month that Dr. Martin Luther King Jr. was celebrated at a biracial dinner, a local intown school changed color overnight. At the time, Kirkwood Elementary School, located in the Kirkwood neighborhood (which is in close proximity to my own neighborhood and actually home to a few of our church's community groups), was barely functioning. The student population had dwindled to almost nothing: 470 children—all white. Meanwhile, the local black schools were suffering with too little space. African American parents pushed for desegregation of the Kirkwood school immediately.

Feeling as though there was little choice, the school board decided to integrate the school, and something remarkable happened in the wake of this decision. Frederick Allen, author of *Atlanta Rising*, writes,

> On the last Friday of January 1965, the school board
> announced that blacks could begin attending classes
> the following Monday.

During the weekend, all but seven of Kirkwood's
white pupils abruptly transferred to other schools. Five
hundred black children arrived on Monday morning
and found they had the place almost completely to
themselves.[12]

Tragically, this narrative, or facets of it, is not uncommon to
many cities in the South. Perhaps it is not uncommon to yours.

Desegregating the Kirkwood school had failed. Desegregating others would follow. At the start of the 1967 school year, the
black student population in Atlanta jumped from 45 percent to
57 percent. A later study found that more than sixty thousand
Anglo Atlantans fled the city between 1960 and 1970.

This trend of what is commonly called white flight did not
cease but continued for decades and with exuberance as shopping malls, office parks, and housing tracts filled almost as
quickly as they were built. The effects on Atlanta cannot be
understated. The rapid expansion of the northern suburbs cost
downtown its preeminence. The central business district, located in downtown Atlanta, dwindled as its share of private
office space shrank from two-thirds to one-sixth of what metro
Atlanta offered. In concert with its losses of office space, the city
also lost its share of retail, service, manufacturing, and other
jobs. These losses only served to intensify both race and class
divisions. The African American population, largely relegated
to the south and southwest of the city, found themselves losing

jobs because of this massive shift. Job loss became key in creating many of the hollowed-out shells scattered throughout the city that were once thriving communities. Significantly, the African Americans who could escape this trend did so. One of the effects of their escapism was the creation of a growing disparity between impoverished African Americans and middle-class and upper-middle-class African Americans that nearly rivals what exists between the Anglos who fled the city and the impoverished African Americans. All of this happened because Maynard Jackson pushed his way to the table and a series of decisions were made to relinquish the city while the city's stabilizers and financial benefactors fled with the money. *But what does any of this have to do with Buckhead?*

Prior to the massive flight of wealthy and primarily white residents from the city of Atlanta, Buckhead was a nice bedroom community. It was known as a "well-to-do white enclave" but little more.[13] This changed in dramatic fashion as, over the years, more than 3.4 million square feet of retail and commercial space was built to serve the most affluent neighborhoods in Georgia. The affluent mall built there also drove the need for both owned and rented high-rise housing, interspersed with dense street-oriented hotels, bars, retail stores, dance clubs, and offices. MARTA stations at two different rail lines and the *only* bus in metro Atlanta that operates at six-minute intervals helped shoppers who couldn't or didn't want to drive to reach the largest, most fashionable selection of goods. The density, high-rises, and mixed-use buildings are classic markers of a city. And yet, Buckhead is no city but simply a part of the one from which it was born. Georgia Tech professor and author Larry Keating captures it best:

> Given the comparatively low levels of retail and housing units in the old city center, Buckhead has clearly supplanted the CBD [central business district] as "Atlanta's white downtown." White dominance in Buckhead is obvious; blacks and other racial minorities are present as service workers or patrons, but not [primarily] as residents. The business of Buckhead is business; there are no government, social, or philanthropic institutions in the area, with the exception of the Atlanta History Center. Regionally, the shift of Atlanta's "center" six miles to the north mirrors the northern expansion of economic and residential activity. One of the most telling points is that the last white mayor of Atlanta, Sam Massell, is known as the (unelected) "mayor" of the relocated and reconstituted white downtown.[14]

Suddenly everything comes into focus. The results of electing an African American mayor, desegregating schools, and the subsequent white flight have reshaped the landscape of the entire city, moving the city center six miles north, because it served the ends of those in control.

THE INCREDIBLE SHRINKING CITY

Though Atlanta boasts of being a world-class city, and in some respects it is, even now only 10 percent of Atlantans actually live within the city limits. What was left in the wake of these mass exoduses and economic shifts was a city desirous of forward progress and regional, if not national, prowess, but in many ways it was unable to accomplish it. Many of the intown neighborhoods deteriorated rapidly in the face of urban development and flight. What were once vibrant urban neighborhoods became pockets of poverty, disparity, and hopelessness. Interstates that were built to assist travel to and from the suburbs contributed to this decline, cutting neighborhoods in half and further isolating struggling communities, cutting them off from the world around them. This is the scene into which God *sent* me and my family.

What looks like rival cities of equal standing from several thousand feet up is actually an illusion. Between the beautiful buildings and skyscrapers of downtown Atlanta, there resides poverty, crime, a lack of resources, and a belief by many that things are unlikely to ever get better. Not so in Buckhead, where the average annual income is $280,631 and the concentration of the economically mobile is visible.

The only departure from this attitude of inner-city resignation is the posture of those now moving back to the city in droves. They are zealous to "reclaim" the city. However, many are purposefully and unwittingly trying to remake the city according to their own vision—one driven by the new chic of city living and all that it has to offer. Much "progress" is made without any consideration given to those already here or the history of that particular neighborhood. Instead of partnering with those who have long labored under the burden of living in densely populated, under-resourced urban areas, these zealots are building their dreams atop the rubble of the shattered lives of people who have struggled to survive in the inner city for multiple generations.

HOW IN THE WORLD?

How in the world could something like the Atlanta/Buckhead divide come to pass? Allow me a little poetic license with Scripture to try to illustrate my point here.

> He also told this parable to some who trusted in themselves that they were righteous, and treated others with contempt: "Two men went up into the temple to pray, one a Pharisee and the other a tax collector. The Pharisee, standing by himself, prayed thus: 'God, I thank you that I am not like other men, extortioners, unjust, adulterers, or even like this tax collector. I fast twice a week; I give tithes of all that I get.' But the tax collector, standing far off, would not even lift up his eyes to heaven, but beat his breast, saying, 'God, be merciful to me, a sinner!' I tell you, this man went down to his house justified, rather than the other. For everyone who

exalts himself will be humbled, but the one who humbles himself will be exalted." (Luke 18:9–14)

Now here are those same verses with a few substitutions:

He also told this parable to some who trusted in themselves that they were righteous, and treated others with contempt. "Two places went up to the temple to pray, one bright and shiny, and the other, well, not so much. The first, a gleaming city prayed thus: 'God, I thank you that I am not like that other place, full of crime and poverty and crumbling infrastructure. I've got great schools and babyGaps.' But the second, a worn-out collection of neighborhoods and businesses, standing far off, would not even lift its eyes to heaven, but just wept, saying, 'God, be merciful to me, full of sin, full of people.' I tell you, there is something about being humbled and something about being exalted, and one of these places gets it and the other won't."

The only way there could be that Atlanta/Buckhead divide, or any such divide in any place, is that there is such a divide in the human heart. You can call it "progress and development" or "ensuring a better life for our children"—call it whatever you like, but I'm calling it "the Pharisee heart." The attitude of that heart says, "Thank God I'm not like him or her or them or there." It is a need to subvert you so I can elevate myself. It is a poison, and poison kills. On the heels of that attitude comes a perversion. You see, I believe we've taken the "go" in the Great Commission of Christ and prostituted it enough to provide us a license to pursue greener pastures somewhere else when things begin to change, otherwise known as when the thrill is gone and things start getting real and messy and human. Jesus had in mind for us to go but then *stay* "and make disciples." Yes, stay. The Great Commission only means something if it is infused with a great compassion.

> Compassion is the sometimes fatal capacity for feeling
> what it's like to live inside somebody else's skin. It is the
> knowledge that there can never really be any peace and
> joy for me until there is peace and joy finally for you too.
> —Frederick Buechner, *Wishful Thinking:*
> *A Seeker's ABC*

PLACE PULSE

We've laid a scriptural foundation for the why of our permanence and the way we should engage God's world. You've read the brief history of my city, my place, in all of its broken beauty. Knowing this history and exploring the present implications of that history has shaped nearly every decision I've made as a husband, father, friend, community leader, and church planter.

So allow me to pose a question: *By what metric do you make your ministry decisions?* If it's not one that allows you to connect theology to reality and past to present, so that you can help shape a preferred future, then how can you trust that you aren't doing more to harm your place than you are doing to help it?

—~~~—

As you're pondering that last question, how about taking your "place pulse." Are you content where you are, in the specific place you live and work? Now I realize we all have bad days, but I'm talking about the general attitude you carry most days. Are you content? Or do you spend most of your waking moments trying to figure out how to get out or break away or just plain leave? Are you always somewhere else in your mind rather than where you actually are in your body?

_____

_____

_____

_____

_____

_____

_____

_____

_____

_____

_____

_____

Three

The Grand Tour

Places matter. Their rules, their scale, their design include or exclude civil society, pedestrianism, equality, diversity (economic and otherwise), understanding of where water comes from and garbage goes, consumption or conservation. They map our lives.

—Rebecca Solnit, *Storming the Gates of Paradise*

I don't know if you've ever seen Atlanta's downtown skyline at night, but it's incredible, almost seeming to have a life of its own. Ever since Breanna and I moved here, we have made a practice of spending time just watching the sun set over our city, noticing where it is we are. There is something magical about it. In each of these moments we feel a tangible connection with this place and the many people who inhabit it.

A few times a week I run down Grant Street past Oakland

Cemetery, heading onto Memorial toward Grant Park. As I run past Augustine's, I think of all the friendships I have made and continue to cultivate there with the owner, bartender, and patrons alike. I dream of a day when maybe, just maybe, they will come to know the hope I have in Jesus and they will share in it with me. But regardless of their decision to follow Jesus or not, I love them because He does. I love them because they are my friends.

As I head farther down Memorial, past Only You Tattoo, Tin Lizzy's, and Ria's Bluebird, I marvel at the culture they have created around good food and community. And I am thankful I have been invited into that. I wave to the servers at Ria's nearly every morning, and they gladly reciprocate.

As I round the park, past all the beautiful Victorian homes and wind back to Memorial, I see the buildings that have yet to experience the renewal effort that has begun in Atlanta and most American cities. I imagine the potential they hold to be places of beauty, culture, education, and, most beautifully, gospel transformation. What if this abandoned warehouse were a place to worship Jesus? What if this empty parking lot were built up to be a place for community education initiatives or an outpost for fighting sex trafficking in the city? How amazing that would be for the glory and fame of Jesus! How amazing that would be for our beloved city!

We love our city. We love where we are. This sentiment has become so familiar in our home that from the age of three, my eldest daughter has routinely said as we walk or drive through downtown, "Look, Daddy, there's our city." Even at three years old she understood the tangible connection we have to this great place and why God sent us to live and serve in the center of the city. This connection we feel comes from the simple call we believe we received on our lives from God: to love this city with gospel intentionality. As often as we stare out over the city, we pray for it. We pray for our neighbors, our city officials, the homeless, and the fatherless. We pray for every diverse grouping of people this city has, and it is both a joy and a privilege to do so.

I trust you noticed the last few paragraphs were full of particulars: Grant Park, Augustine's, Ria's Bluebird. They are specific to my place, my city. Here's an exercise for you, one I hope you'll pause and take the time to do. Imagine I paid you a visit and asked you to take me on a walk or a drive, a kind of grand tour of the place—city or town—God has sent you.

- Where would you take me? Could we walk?
  Or would we need to drive?
- What would you show me? Be as specific as you
  can, full of particulars. What history would you
  absolutely ensure I was familiar with?
- Would our pace be fast? Could we finish in a
  couple of hours? Or would it take quite a bit of
  time?

There are three postures we typically take toward our place: we choose to be *of, against,* or *for.* The kind of tour you give me would tell me a lot about your posture toward your place.

THE LONG ROAD TO ATLANTA

There was not a single human reason in the world why I would have come back to Atlanta. I'd spent some time here in 2004 as I pursued a short-lived NFL career, but I had no earthly reason to return. In 2006 I made a terrible mistake; I began reimagining the church and all that it could be. I also had one of the strangest dreams I've ever had. At first I wasn't sure if it was a bad dinner or the Holy Spirit, so I gave it some time. But ultimately it led me to sit down and begin to write out what was missing from the church. If there had been a headline, it would have been this:

> The church should be God's redemptive agent in the world and nothing less.

I folded up that piece of paper and stuck it in a book I happened to be reading at the time. Fast forward to 2007. I'd begun blogging my thoughts, and somehow some of them came across the desk of a principal at an executive firm hired by one of the large churches in Atlanta.

He and I began to communicate about a potential role for a church planter in a large organization in the Southeast. Little did I know that in the process of our communication I was one of three hundred candidates. All our conversations and subsequent interviews eventually led to a face-to-face meeting with the leadership of the church in Atlanta. The interview went well for the first three hours, and then we hit a sticking point. Here is a summary of that conversation.

Me: So, will your lead pastor be on the screen preaching?

Them: Yes.

Me: The people I'm trying to reach won't listen to him.

Them: Who are you trying to reach?

Me: The church should encompass the full breadth of God's creative genius.

Them: Our target is reaching eighteen- to forty-year-olds.

Me: I want that too, but I don't want them to look the same or have the same background. I want it to be fully reflective of everybody.

Them: We're not interested in that.

Me: Well, you're not interested in me.

But my heart was burdened more than ever for church planting. As Breanna and I were driving back home, we hopped on University and got turned around and wound up on Hank Aaron, and it was right there, in Grant Park, that the Holy Spirit said, *This is the place where you'll give your life.* I began to sweat with fear and anticipation. I didn't say anything to Breanna. I just let the feeling pass, and we drove on home. But that line—*This is the place where you'll give your life*—never left me.

Early one morning, about two weeks later, Breanna woke

me up and said, "I think we're called to Atlanta." I said, "Excuse me?" then turned over and went back to sleep. Later that morning I was trying to be playful with her, and she would have none of it. I finally asked, "What's your deal?" She looked me in the eye and said, "You know what God told you." After that confirmation, which I wisely heeded, I decided we would fast and pray to see if this was really from the Lord. And God began to open doors. Well, slowly.

We moved our family into the mattress factory lofts in Atlanta, began to learn our neighbors, and built a core group (our second) that gathered in our home. From September 2008 to February 2009, I applied for 187 jobs and did not get one of them. Not one. At the same time, the core group gathered in our home began to dissipate. Out of our initial group of thirty people, twenty-seven moved away. By January 2009 I was sure I had missed God—somehow all the doors that had opened to that point were in fact not signs of God's providence but a misinterpretation of events. I'd been wrong. And we were left with nothing.

With only thirty-five dollars in the bank, our rent due, and everything that could be pawned pawned, I guessed we had only one option—move into my parents' home. I needed to figure out my next move. I reached a depth of despair that can only be described as hopeless. No people, no money, no vision—I couldn't imagine anything ever coming to pass. I'll never forget standing at the window of that third-floor loft, crying and looking out on a snowy Atlanta, wondering where things had gone so wrong. I distinctly remember my wife came and hugged me, kissed my face, and said, "Léonce, we'll be okay. You've got to believe. God sent us here. This is where we're supposed to be. God sent us here, and He's not going to leave us."

Shortly after this tender moment, I received a phone call from an acquaintance who told me they were getting ready to multiply their church and I was the guy to lead it. The offer on the table was a condo on the beach and a very generous salary, plus people committed from his sending church. When I told him I felt God's call to Atlanta, he asked me how things were going. I was honest. I told him about being jobless, how we had lost almost our entire core group, and how we had pawned all our stuff. He said, "It sounds like nothing's working. Maybe Atlanta is just a stop on the way to somewhere else."

Press the Pause button here. Now, not always, but many times that statement is a perfect reflection of the transient attitude that plagues our world. Yes, sometimes it is time to move on. But more often it's time to wait and watch.

Okay, back to the story. I promised him I'd pray about it, but his offer sent me into an inner turmoil. All my doubts became an army of shouting confirmations that Atlanta was just a thoroughfare. But in the midst of all this was Breanna. My wife would not relent. She was convinced Atlanta was for us. "Léonce, I love you, and I'll follow you anywhere, but I feel if we leave Atlanta, we'll be disobeying God."

I called Kathy Dobson, a good friend and spiritual mother,

and asked her to pray with and for me. She called back a couple of days later and said: "Son, take this for what it's worth. I saw you walking through what looked like a corridor, and in your hand there was a small seed. You walked to a crossroads, took out a hammer and broke the concrete there, made a small hole, then dropped that seed into it. You knelt down and began to pray and weep over that seed. I looked and nothing was happening. Then a little shoot popped up, and you began to pray more. And as you prayed, you wept, and that little shoot became a great vine and that vine began to cover everything. It just kept spreading. I don't know what that means to you, but I think it's pretty clear where God has called you." I hung up the phone and shared Kathy's words with my wife. Breanna said, "See, God wants us in Atlanta. God's gonna make a way. He'll make a way for us to stay here."

After that day my heart turned. I don't know how; it just did. I knew God was going to work things out, that He was calling us to plant not only a church but ourselves.

A week or so later I went to a work/faith conference here in Atlanta, and I ran into the same principal from the executive firm that got me the interview with the large church in Atlanta. He asked what I was doing, and I gave him the whole story, including the piece about not being able to find work. Long story short is that he got me another interview, this time with FaithBridge Foster Care. They were recruiting past and present pastors as case workers. After sailing through the interview, I got the job. That began an upswing in our life here in Atlanta.

One day before our eviction process began, I was able to pay our rent. Ministry efforts in our neighborhood began to gain more traction. We began to gather new people into our small loft. And for the first time in many months, it felt like I'd heard correctly from God after all.

JUST A CITY BOY

Now, you may be thinking this is nothing more than a book by someone who just loves the city, and in particular, Atlanta. I do love the city; it would be a fiction to claim I don't. But I also love that which is not-the-city: places like towns and suburbs, wards and unincorporated areas. In fact, everything I needed to know about ministry in Atlanta, Georgia, I learned in a small place known as Sevierville, Tennessee.

EVERYTHING I NEEDED TO KNOW

What? You're not familiar with Sevierville? Well, have you ever seen a pit bull walking down the street carrying a two-by-four in his mouth, followed by a guy with nothing on but overalls? No? Well I have. In fact, that was one of my first images of Sevierville. It is a small town northeast of Knoxville, a place you drive through in order to get somewhere else. For most people, that somewhere else is the popular tourist destination known as Gatlinburg. For many residents, Sevierville was the place where criminals hide and dreams die. But this also was the place where God would teach me everything. Yes, everything I needed to know about the gospel's ability to change anyone, alter everything, and make a family of any group of people. And I learned it all far from the skyline of a city.

In 2007, shortly after Breanna and I married, I met Tom Sterbens, a dynamic ministry leader who had moved up from Florida to take over the leadership of New Hope Church. Tom could hold anyone's attention because of the intellectual nature with which he communicated the gospel. When I met Tom, he shared his dream of moving his church beyond the borders of Sevierville. His desire was to start a college ministry in Knoxville, which would eventually birth a city expression of New Hope Church. The idea of church planting was just beginning to bloom in my heart. In fact, I thought about it constantly. It sounded like an incredible opportunity. After many conversations, we decided that though it seemed far and away different from every opportunity we had in front of us at the time (Houston, New York, Miami), we felt God was sending us to Sevierville.

When we first arrived, we were struck by the number of barbecue restaurants. And the vastness of the land, scarcely populated by people. We got settled in an apartment that happened to be just down the street from Dolly Parton's multiacre ranch. We got to work on a very steep learning curve. New Hope was a fast-growing rural church. They had just bought the Lee Greenwood Theater, and it was filling up every week. Among my responsibilities—teaching classes, benevolence—I was responsible for seeing the college ministry grow. At my first "meeting," it was I and four young adults, only one of them actually in college. The five of us talked and dreamed about what God could do. Truth be told, I was fairly certain this would never work.

DEEPER THAN BLACK AND WHITE

The first lesson I learned in Sevierville is that people are people no matter where they grew up, how much money they have, or how many degrees hang on the wall. People have hurts, fears, hopes, dreams, wounds, and aspirations for something better, even if they can't quite see what that is. That understanding, and it was gradual, became the foundation for everything we did going forward. It allowed us to hurdle all our differences. I was a black kid from urban Louisiana, and these were people whose only experiences with any ethnic minority were via television. Sevierville was 95.88 to 99 percent white.

But in addition to people being people, there is a particular way people receive what you're saying. After the initial pleasantries, this small band of four, plus me, started to meet weekly as a group. Within just a few weeks our group started to show some promise and steadily gain some new faces. It was exciting, particularly because I'd felt over my head when I first engaged these folks in this context. Now that we had some traction, I believed we might just make it work—but that feeling soon disintegrated into self-doubt. Why? For as long as I could remember, I had been told I was a gifted communicator. But all of a sudden that giftedness went straight out the window. I'd get up to teach, and it seemed like I was staring at white paint in an undecorated room. I'd ask my wife, "Was I unclear? Off? What?"

Eventually I realized Breanna understood me because we spoke the same language. People are the same at the core, but the way they interpret life is specific to the soil from which they sprouted. I began to see how foreign my language was. I had an epiphany: If I could not speak their language, it wouldn't matter what I was saying. Instead of taking the approach of most ministers that it's the people who need to change, I realized instead it was me who needed changing.

I became a voracious student of rural culture. I began to listen regularly to country music—Great American Country and Country Music Television. I watched the Blue Collar Comedy Tour and *Reba,* started mountain biking, gigging, and hanging out at the river. I began to pick up on local colloquialisms and even added some twang. I began making the transition from alien urbanite who came to save Sevierville to being "one of them." I wasn't *above* but *among.* When I allowed myself that, then I was able to reach them and *be* reached in return.

I'll always remember the sermon I preached about the great storm on the sea. The disciples were looking for Jesus, the storm raged, and fear struck their hearts. Then they saw Jesus walking across the water. Jesus said, "Peter, come out on the water." Where I would have usually made a reference to something urbane or unnecessarily intellectual, I shifted and referenced the

Blue Collar Comedy Tour instead. When I saw their blank stares, I said, "Well, you know Peter, he was like Larry the Cable Guy—git-r-done." *Boom.* I saw the spark in their eyes. They were with me, on a level place where they understood me because I understood them, and we understood the gospel together. Some might call this connection, but I believe it was communion. All of a sudden my little group of four began to multiply rapidly. I was no longer a Louisianan but a Seviervillian. I realize that sounds a little Dr. Seuss, but the reality is, that's what happened. There was really nothing novel about this approach; it was the one Jesus used when He set aside His glory and came as one of us. Incarnation is the primary means of meaningful ministry. It's the bedrock of place making.

The final lesson I learned in Sevierville is that the gospel can change everything and connect anyone, even people like me and James Smith. James had been in and out of our ministry for some time. He'd been a part of New Hope for a long time and had lived a rough life. He began dealing meth and using meth, landing him in the church's rehab program. But since he was college-age, he was pushed toward the college ministry. He was the poster child for Sevierville: Carhartts, mud boots, gun rack. Every stereotype, he had it. The few times he graced us with his presence, he would sit in the back, fold his arms, and quickly leave when the service ended. But one night he sat close to the front. I could tell he was locked into what I was saying. At the end of the gathering, he came and asked if he could speak to me a few minutes. He proceeded to tell me,

"I can't call ya nigger on account of what God done in my heart, and my granddad says that the proper thing to call you is colored to be respectful-like, but I figured I'd ask you before I called you anything." I smiled and said, "That's a fine idea. You can call me Pastor or Léonce or Pastor Léonce." We had a brief moment, looking at each other, realizing a friendship was birthed there that homogeneous unit principles would dismiss. James stuck out his hand to shake my hand, and I shook his. "Well, hell, Pastor, I'm on your team." Even though he still had struggles after that, James was my right-hand man in Sevierville. I got to see the gospel do amazing things in his life. The gospel can change everything and connect anyone. Sevierville is proof of that. James and I are proof of that. Yes, everything I needed to know about the gospel's ability to change anyone, alter everything, and make a family of any group of people, I learned in Sevierville, Tennessee:

1. People are people.

2. If you can't speak someone's language, it doesn't matter what you're saying.

3. The gospel can change everything and connect anyone.

―――

Chances are good you can read my three lessons from Sevierville and nod your head in agreement. But if you had to choose one that you're particularly wrestling with these days, which one would it be and why? What's the story behind the struggle? Answer that question, and I promise you, your ministry, whatever its nature, will never be the same. The fruit on the other side is worth the work.

_____

_____

_____

_____

_____

_____

_____

_____

_____

_____

_____

_____

_____

_____

_____

_____

_____

_____

_____

_____

_____

A Round-Table Discussion

PL: Hello. I'm Pastor Léonce Crump, and I'm here with a few of my friends—brothers I love dearly—and we're going to have a conversation about this new urban renewal movement. And if we have time, we'll apply it to the basic ideas of how you move into a neighborhood, what the transformation of a neighborhood looks like, what it means to be a good neighbor, and how the gospel can be applied to all peoples and to all places. So fellas, if you would introduce yourselves before we launch into this.

MA: Matt Armstrong, pastor of Village Church here in East Atlanta.

WA: Will Ampong. I've been in Atlanta since 2001.

LM: Lecrae Moore. I'm an artist, and I've been in Atlanta about five years now.

PL: Well, guys, I am glad you would take the time to join me. Let's launch right into it. Give me your initial thoughts on this new urban renewal movement, this kind of thrust back into the cities. And then, specifically, this idea that the church is supposed to be leading the way in making communities better by seeing them transformed. What are your initial thoughts on that?

LM: I think historically, you know, we've seen churches specifically from a wealthier social class feel a social responsibility to engage or to affect lower-income communities that are predominantly in an urban location. A lot of that looked like driving in, doing something, then driving back out. Driving in, doing something, then driving back out. Then, over time, we've seen, and I don't think this was a church deal, we've seen people from majority-white suburban contexts moving back into cities and starting to thrive in those cities. And we've seen the church say, "So this is looking advantageous or safer, now we can come in here alongside them in the name of the social justice mission work." But it's been kinda like, "Hey, we are making this community thrive, but we're also building things that we like as well." That's what I feel like we are seeing now. Some of what is happening has been beneficial, and some of what is happening has been detrimental.

PL: Will, do you want to volley off that?

WA: I think as you start to see the transition of people moving from suburbs to urban communities, like you said, it's getting more appealing. The rub I see is that you have people who want to live in urban communities and renew those communities, but the by-product of that is almost eliminating the people that already live there. So the question is, How can I make my community better but still make it a place that the people that have been living here for decades before me can still live in?

It sounds great to get a group of people to move into this neighborhood to change it. But in making all those changes you end up excluding the community itself from reaping the benefits of those changes. Because now it's an environment that they can't live in, they can't thrive in. The result is people that live in the community aren't *from* the community, and so the changes are going to be reflective of them. The changes you see in that community are going to be influenced by people that really don't have a stake in it, at least they haven't had. And so how do you wrestle with those two things? How do you truly change a community while still maintaining the complexion of the community?

PL: I know, for me, this idea of moving back in has been complicated to discern and wrestle with because when you look at the social patterns from city to suburban over the last several decades, there was a massive flight all at once in Atlanta. You know the 1960s were called the greatest decade in the history of

Atlanta. Yet at the same time, in that ten years, some seventy thousand, mostly white but also some wealthy or upwardly mobile African Americans, moved out of the city and into the suburbs.

Matt, I'd like to get your ideas on this. What if we go in and ask questions before doing anything? What if, before we made a move to start anything, build anything, launch anything, or open anything, we just spent time there being neighbors, getting to know the people who have already invested there for ten, fifteen, even twenty years? Do you think that will make a big difference in how neighborhoods transition, change, and grow?

LM: Absolutely! I think asking questions must be primary. That demonstrates empathy.

PL: And humility.

LM: Humility, as well as trying to step into someone else's shoes and saying, "Man, how can I serve you?" rather than "How can I do what I think is best for you?" To me that eliminates coming into the city saying, "Look at all these fried chicken shacks everywhere! This is terrible for people to eat! You know, I'm gonna build an organic submarine sandwich shop, and then they can have subs that are good for them." Well, you didn't ask if anybody in the community likes subs, though.

PL: Or wanted them.

LM: Or wanted them. Instead, maybe you develop a relationship with Ms. Jenkins down the street, and you ask her about what she likes. And then you and Ms. Jenkins start an organic chicken shack. You know what I mean? And maybe that's the way to do it, asking those questions to understand the community, understanding who the people are that you are trying to serve. Not just coming in with an imperialistic kind of mentality that says, "I know what's best for you, so let me help you out. Here you go." I think that definitely demonstrates humility.

PL: I want to come back to that idea of imperialism. But first I want to hear from my brother Matt, who lives here in the city. You didn't grow up in the city, did you?

MA: No, the suburbs of Atlanta.

PL: So what was the drive for you to move back to the city? What were you hoping to see in that effort?

MA: Yeah, as I hear you describe this cultural trend, I think I was just part of it. I think people grew tired with things in the suburbs—the monotony, the sprawl, the distance, the isolation. So there was something that was both healthy and chic about moving back to the city where there's unique restaurants, you are close to your neighbors, you can walk places, and it's not a twenty-minute drive everywhere.

So there are plenty of Christians moving into the city. We've done this for hundreds of years. This is nothing new. We'll move into a community, and it's like "We've got what you need. Convert or die." That's the old way of putting it. But what's complicated is non-Christians who move into the city for these cultural movements have no real reason to care for their neighbors. They want to build the sub shop because that's what they want. If their neighbor is poor and a nuisance, they want them gone.

PL: I want to hit on something briefly, and I don't want to be provocative just for the sake of being provocative, but it's something you just said. We do understand that the people who are not Christians are gonna move in. They're gonna have selfish ends. I've experienced this in this very neighborhood, which has slowly gentrified over the last seven years since I moved to Atlanta in 2008. The night we moved into our loft, someone got murdered across the street in what is now called Augustine's. It used to be the Standard bar. It wasn't uncommon for us to hear automatic gunfire at night and hear the lions at the zoo in the morning. And that was the strange tension we existed in. My wife and I have seen this neighborhood go through this bumpy transition along the lines of the rise and fall of the housing market, and what has remained is the tension of gentrification.

I also want to address something you alluded to, that the church is not supposed to follow the traditional route. Yet what I've seen, and if I'm being too judgmental, then you guys push back, because this is an open dialogue, but from what I've seen, the church has done more to follow suit than it has to lead the way or to change the conversation, at least in our context. I'd like to get your thoughts on that. What do you think?

MA: Yeah, I don't think I can disagree with that.

WA: I agree. And it seems like the church, they want to see renewal, but they want to keep it at arm's length.

PL: Explain that. I think that's a great idea to chase.

WA: So let's say I am a Christian that wants to renew my neighborhood and my community. I really want to, but I want to be able to turn it off at night. So all these people around me, I'm going to go and help. I'm going to go to their house, I'm going to give them a turkey on Thanksgiving, and I'm going to invite them to my Bible study. But on Sunday, when it's time to watch a football game, I'm going to bring my other friends in. So I think if you really want to see a renovating kind of renewal, you have to be *all in* to the community. And that's not just on Sundays or during your weekly meetings or whatever. I think this means the school systems, the economy, the businesses, every aspect of the community—you have to be *all in*. And I feel like

Christians in particular want to see renewal for the gospel's sake but not necessarily for the city's sake.

PL: So you want to dig into that a little bit?

WA: Yeah. My experience with Christians, and I didn't grow up with Christianity in my life—

PL: Yeah, give us a little bit of your background. I think it's interesting.

WA: So I grew up in New England. My mom is from a Catholic background, but she's not really a practicing Catholic. My dad is from West Africa, where religion is very perverted. They believe that people can get turned into goats and what not. So they came together, and I grew up with no concept of Christianity. No concept of religion. So it sometimes baffles me when you get in church circles and people assume that everybody knows the story of the gospel. Because I'll tell you that they don't. I learned it in college. I didn't know who Jesus was. I knew the name, had some friends named Jésus, but I didn't know Jesus. And so I was always on the other side of that coin, where I was always a project for people. I would meet people, particularly in college where you have groups with similar interests banding together. They would say, "Hey, man, you want to come play basketball? Okay, cool. You want to go play video games? All right, now let me tell you about Jesus." That gave me a bad taste in my mouth, that these people don't generally want me in their life.

PL: It felt agenda driven.

WA: Yeah, so I feel like, in the church, the renewal is often agenda driven. I want to see renewal for the gospel's sake but probably more so that I can please God. There's not a true desire for renewal in the people you're trying to reach. The stance has too often been that I want to please God. It is something that the gospel called me to do. But all these nameless people? I don't know that I really want a relationship with them.

LM: I agree with that. I think a large part of what Will is saying is that we, the church, have got to consider how we talk about cultural engagement. We've got to consider really stepping into the culture and becoming a part of it.

PL: [Sarcastically] But what if it gets on me though? (Laughter)

LM: It needs to get on you, and what the Scriptures reject is what you reject. But I mean, it's ironic to me that when we go to a foreign country we understand that we've got to adopt some things. I've got to dress differently. I've got to come to grips with the fact that I'm going to eat different food now for the rest of my life. I'm going to have to speak a new language. I'm going to have to understand new customs. But in our own backyard we say, "No, no, no, no. I don't want to change that much about me. I just want you to come and adapt and assimilate to what I have going on." And I think if you consider yourself a missionary, specifically in the urban context, then you've got to adjust and adapt and embrace some aspects of that culture in order to really influence and affect it. Similar to Will, I didn't grow up in the church, and I had a guy who was way outside my cultural context befriend me in order to connect with me. He asked me what kind of movies I watched. What kinds of songs I liked. And he would sit there and watch these movies. And he didn't know nothing about *Boyz in the Hood* or *Menace II Society*. He didn't know anything about hip-hop, but he would sit there listening to this, just trying to understand who I was.

PL: He didn't have no baby O-Dog braids?

LM: He didn't know about O-Dog. And that's a cultural icon for me. (Laughter) Even to this day that's an aspect of cultural engagement, and I think it's expected when we leave this country. But in our own backyard? As Will said, we want it at arm's length. We don't want to embrace all that.

PL: Here's a question for you, Matt. You're a pastor, robustly theologically trained, so tell us, can we desire renewal for an individual and it be completely without agenda to the point where we want Atlanta to prosper whether all Atlantans become Christians or not?

MA: Yeah.

PL: So what we're saying is that we want to see the city thrive. We want to contribute to the thriving of the city, to the thriving of our neighborhoods, to the thriving of our neighbors, to the complete flourishing of humanity, whether they ever become Christians or not. But we always desire for them to become Christians.

MA: Sure.

PL: But we will not relent in our efforts just because they don't hear our gospel.

MA: Yeah, I think either Paul or Peter tells us to pray for peace so we can live quiet lives. And he connects that to the gospel. He wants people to come to faith, perhaps because political unrest and lack of flourishing gets in the way of people considering the gospel. The other side of that coin is that it's great if our neighbor thrives and makes their way up the economic chain, but it's not great if that neighbor goes to hell. For evangelicals, that's a big deal. But we also believe in what the Fall did to the world and to individuals, and someone being mistreated or bullets flying through someone's windows is not the way it's supposed to be.

PL: So you believe the gospel has social implications?

MA: Sure, of course. But here's something. I know of well-meaning affluent Caucasians who move into the inner city, and they want to be *all in*. But a year or two later they leave, retreat. They're deeply wounded, hurt, whatever word fits. Because, and this is complicated, they didn't achieve their predetermined understanding of renewal. They didn't know how long it would really take. And what it would really take.

PL: They don't count the cost.

WA: But what does that approach really change? That's just "Here's what you guys need" or "Here is how you can be like me" or "Here is how you can replicate my path to success."

MA: You mean, what does actual cultural renewal take? Or why do some of these people get burned out?

WA: Some of these people get burned out because they're just offering the path they followed. But that may not be effective for the people they're trying to help.

LM: I don't even know if that's an urban or a culturally urban thing as much as a missionary approach. People leave other countries and say, "That junk is hard. I'm not seeing the fruit that I want to see." I think that's why the Scriptures tell us not to grow weary in doing good. This is tough work.

PL: It is tough work, and I think one of the primary issues with seeing that work through to some sense of satisfaction is an underrealized understanding of cultural renewal. It's an escapism mentality that's been taught in the church. I'm not interested in a rapture debate, but basically this doctrine teaches that we're going to escape this place, the world. And if we're going to get out of here, then our only real goal is to get as many people saved as we possibly can, and then we'll all get out of here. So forget any kind of a long-range view, whether for a neighborhood or an urban or suburban setting. It'll all be destroyed in some fashion at some point, so let's just get as many people on the bus as we can. But what if God intends to restore this world? What if we are home? That would change how we view renewal. I recently made the statement that if God does not intend to restore the world that He made and called very good in Genesis, then either He is too weak to rid the world of sin or too fickle to uphold His covenant that He made with creation. If He does intend to reclaim His world, then everything is long-range. Everything. If that is true, it changes the game of renewal.

MA: Yeah, I appreciate that. One of the most helpful metaphors for me came from Eugene Peterson in *Eat This Book*. He was talking about all of this. It's about the farmer and the farm. The farmer has far more to do than he can do in a day, and so the result, ironically, is that he doesn't rush. He knows he can't do it all today. He only knows what needs to be done today, and so he does that. He also knows that what he does today will not bear fruit for possibly months. But he takes the long view, and tilling, planting, watering, it's all a part of it. If you look at his workday today, he looks slow, even pointless.

PL: Ineffective.

MA: Ineffective. Like, what are you doing with your time? But the farmer knows how things work.

LM: That's funny. Parents use that same approach with their kids. I've got a seven-year-old. I'm not trying to teach him to be a twenty-one-year-old in a day. There is an urgency for him to be responsible and to be able to take care of himself. But we're taking our time, taking the long view. It would be ridiculous to say, "Learn all the nuances of driving today."

PL: It would be ridiculous. So what is it that keeps us from considering ministry in the same way? Is it a need for success? To make a name for ourselves? Pressure? I know that Breanna and I lived here for three years before there was a Renovation Church. It took three failed attempts at getting started, and three core-group blowups in church-planting language. I soon realized God wasn't gonna let me start any other way. But there was extreme pressure to do something rather than just be present with the people. People asked, "What are you doing down there?" and "When are you starting services?"

MA: When are we going to get a return on our investment?

PL: Yes. When are we going to get a return on our investment? Honestly, it wasn't until the last eight months before we actually launched a service that I began to rest in the fact that being present with the people was the ministry I was supposed to be doing, and that if I was faithful in that, then God would teach me by way of this neighborhood how it would hear the gospel. Any thoughts on that?

MA: What I like about the story is that it wasn't because you figured it all out. You were trying. You wanted to achieve, like we all do. And God graciously squashed those plans in order to teach you His plan is the one being played out, not yours. It's too often about our plan, our agenda, and not God's. But if it's His plan, then the pressure is really off in a lot of ways. We still have to be faithful in day-by-day fashion, but at the end of the day, it's God's story.

PL: Lecrae, you're an artist. I have personally watched the transition in your life take place from the pressure to be everybody's musical pastor to, and I'll say this very tongue-in-cheek, your very Kuyperian view of what it is you do now. How do you view making good music, not necessarily Christian music, but good music that espouses a clear biblical worldview? And let me set the table for that with something I said a few weeks ago that biblical, or scriptural, knowledge and a biblical worldview are not the same thing. A biblical worldview is being able to interpret the culture through what you believe about the Scriptures. How do you see that playing out in your artistry and even in the, some would say, directional change in what you're doing?

LM: I started making music that was answer-driven. I needed to give answers to the questions. The objective was not to make great art but answer the questions I felt the culture was asking. So I was making hip-hop, giving answers, and that's all the cultural engagement I thought I needed. But I learned quickly that we do not live in the Christianized nation we think we live in.

PL: Christendom is over.

LM: Right! Within a church we still believe the world understands Christianese. I remember someone asking me, "Are you saved?" and I had no idea what she was talking about. I was, like, "What are you saying to me?"

PL: That was probably the first Christian conversation I ever had. Just for context, I grew up a bad Catholic. No Christian understanding.

MA: Me too.

PL: I went to an all-black Catholic church. That really exists. But I remember hearing the same thing: "Hey, man, are you saved?" And I'm, like, "From what? I don't see any dogs. I don't see any guns."

LM: But that's the point. What I had to learn in creating good art or music was to raise great questions and tell great stories. That's the ambition for me as I engage with culture. I don't feel the pressure to give answers in every song. If it comes, it comes. A lot of those great questions are in the stories I'm telling through the biblical narrative.

PL: I would say all of them are. Just because you're not quoting Scripture when you exalt and elevate marriage doesn't mean you don't espouse a biblical worldview. You don't have to quote a thousand scriptures to do that.

LM: A thousand scriptures and giving answers to questions people aren't even asking.

PL: Yes.

LM: There is art that is for the church, and there is art that is from the church. I think all of it should be phenomenal. All of it should be phenomenal. We live in a time where Mormon temples and Buddhist statues are done with incredible craftsmanship because they see a reverence that should go into that, and for us Christians, we say it's not about that, it's just about the answer. Like as long as there is a cross, it doesn't have to be a pretty one.

PL: Which is a change, which is a major change. And through that, cultural renewal is happening.

LM: That's the long-term vision. That's the now and that's the then—to create great lasting art that pushes back darkness and brings in light with, you know, just the content reflecting the kingdom.

PL: Yeah!

LM: As you were saying before, it does say something about my eschatology. It does say a lot about—

PL: *Eschatology*? I want everybody to know you used that word. I did not. (Laughter)

MA: He used it well.

PL: He did use it well. Go ahead. You use that word.

LM: Listen, all I'm saying is that, at the end of the day, I do believe that we are demonstrating what the kingdom looks like, and that is why I want to make great art. I want to see beauty and transformation happen. I don't believe in utopian thinking—that we're going to get it all right now. But I believe that God is using us to demonstrate what it is going to look like.

PL: Well, it's the already-not-yet. Jesus said the kingdom broke in.

MA: I just want to jump in and commend that move. And I'm sure that God is maturing you and discipling you. The art you made five, ten years ago was the art you needed to make.

LM: Absolutely!

PL: Yes!

MA: You were answering the questions you were asking. The reason you had a following is because other people were asking those questions. But we're talking about incarnational ministry. Here is what I see. I was trained in Van Tillian apologetics, and Van Til taught that, look, we know the gospel is true. We know God exists, and we actually know non-Christians know God exists. But we also know that unbelievers suppress the truth actively. And so they deny the existence of God or the existence of the triune God, whatever. So the way he taught apologetics, here is how you do apologetics that is faithful to Scripture. You never bend on the truth, but you're not going to beat someone over the head with it. They are actively suppressing it. So what you do is you go to their ground and begin asking questions. You begin to relate. Say, "I know you struggle in your marriage. I know you struggle with work. I know you struggle with purpose. I know you put on a facade. I know you're worried, and that in the middle of the night you wake up in a cold sweat. Guess what, so do I."

PL: I know "you are greater than the songs you creating."

LM: Some guy wrote that.

PL: Some guy said that.

MA: Sorry, I'm showing my irrelevance here.

LM: Right now we're talking Van Tillian apologetics.

MA: I got to drop his name because nobody knows it. But that is exactly what you're doing. You are now taking the biblical foundational worldview that you have, and that you believe, but you're bringing it to a broader audience by asking the questions they're asking. And it's good art. On its face. On its own. But it has the dual benefit of reaching a broader audience.

PL: That's your new defense: "I'm doing Van Tillian apologetics." Listen, we're running out of time, so I want to ask two last questions here. The first one, we've talked all around it, but I want to get a succinct answer from each of you. How do you transform a community? I'll start with you, Pastor.

MA: The first short answer I have to give is that nobody transforms a community. God transforms the community. We are God's fellow workers, so we have a role to play in that. And I would say if you want to change, you have to respect the culture that was there before you. And respect, even if you have been there the whole time, that it took years and decades for that culture to form. And so if culture is actually going to change in a way that is beneficial to all, it's going to take a long time.

PL: That is beautiful. Crae?

LM: Trying to keep it simple, obviously it's been stated: God does the work. But I think it's learning the people, learning that culture, learning them in humility. Empathy, as Cornel West said, is not just caring or trying to put yourself in their shoes. It's actually taking yours off and walking in their shoes to get them out of their situation. To genuinely love people is to step in to sacrifice, to be selfless, to bring the light of Jesus.

PL: That sounds a lot like John 1, the incarnation. Is that the biblical worldview thing showing up again?

LM: Yeah. I've read that a couple of times I think, in my life, maybe. I think—learning the people, loving the people.

PL: Stepping in.

LM: Yeah, and I think that's really where you're going to see God beginning to do some work. If you genuinely, and I don't mean to sound condescending or patronizing when I say like being a parent, because I'm not saying we are parents to these communities, but I am saying it's the same way I hope to engage my kids. I want to learn them in humility. And then I want to love them well. And hopefully that brings forth the transformation that God provides.

WA: I think both are good points. The gospel is the way, and loving people is also the way.

PL: Yeah, that's exactly right.

WA: If it's always "You need to be a Christian before I'm going to help you" or "This guy, he's not receptive to the gospel. He's a lost cause. I'm gonna go to this family over here"—I think you can remove that from your day-to-day approach with your community. I think that's the way to go.

LM: That's very Christian. Whether you want it to be or not.

PL: It is Christian. It's just not the churchianity that most of us have been privy to. The last thing I want to ask is, Is this applicable in the suburbs? We talked a lot about the city, but the readers of *Renovate,* the watchers of this conversation will be multifaceted. They will be global watchers in Kenya and Australia, South Africa, in America, in urban contexts, suburban contexts. Are these ideas applicable to any place, any people?

MA: They have to be.

WA: Absolutely!

LM: You see it in the Bible, so absolutely yeah.

A Theology of Place

When a Navajo baby is born, the parents bury the umbilical cord somewhere on the property near where their *Hogan,* or house, sits.

Why? So that the baby is always connected to the place it came from.

—Dr. Richard Twiss

PRODUCTS OF PLACE

Holidays in the Crump home are a balancing act. My wife and I not only differ ethnically, but culturally as well. (Please note those are not the same thing.) With our differences come the gymnastics routine we do every holiday to try to complement each other's tastes and memories. For example, my wife's memories are of gigantic family gatherings, at least three generations, complete with aunts, cousins, and everyone in between. They always ate "traditional" holiday food: turkey, stuffing, cranberry sauce, pumpkin pie, french green beans, and salad.

They never ever had a salad-free meal. This is all she ever knew as a California girl.

I, on the other hand, cannot recall a single Thanksgiving or Christmas where we ate any of those things, except turkey, and even it was deep-fried. I'm from the great state of Louisiana, and we rarely do anything traditionally. If you've ever been to New Orleans, you know this. If you've ever experienced the sights and sounds of Mardi Gras, it's likely you've already been captivated by the wonder that is my home. Unlike my wife's family, our holiday meals were always anchored by a giant pot of gumbo. The smell of fresh seafood and andouille sausage would fill the house for days, long after the cooking was done. We ate cornbread dressing, not stuffing. And I had never eaten french green beans or cranberry sauce until I was married.

My wife and I are both products of the places from which we come. Her family has been in California since her great-grandparents moved there. My family has been in Louisiana since before the Emancipation Proclamation. And each of us is unmistakably tied to those places, not only by origin, but by accent, culture, and allegiance to everything that defines our respective homes. You should see us when the Saints play the Niners—yeah, it isn't pretty.

Even though I've been gone from Louisiana for nearly fifteen years (except my brief stint playing football for the Saints), every time I return home, there is an ever-expanding sense of warmth and excitement as soon as we cross the state line. Why?

Because human beings are not only uniquely tied to the people they love but also to the places they inhabit. When they leave those places, it often creates an unspoken sense of longing that is difficult to put into words. But *place* captures our individual cultures, keeps safe our memories, binds us as a people, and gives that sense of belonging as much or more than anything else in the world.

Place can seem to be an abstract concept. In fact, geographer David Harvey asserts that the term *place* has an extraordinary range of metaphorical meanings. "We talk about the place of art in social life, the place of women in society, our place in the cosmos, and we internalize such notions psychologically in terms of knowing our place, or feeling we have a place in the affection or esteem of others."[15] But these metaphorical meanings, although they have become societal norms, do not capture the true nature of *place* and its ability to define so many of our cultural expressions and intimate feelings.

Geographer Yi-Fu Tuan explains the human orientation with *place,* saying,

> The infant acquires a sense of distance by attending to
> the sound of a human voice that signals the approach of
> his mother. A child is walked to school a few times and
> thereafter he can make the trip on his own, without
> the help of a map; indeed, he is unable to envisage the
> route. We are in a strange part of town: unknown space

stretches ahead of us. In time we know a few landmarks and the routes connecting them. Eventually what was strange town and unknown space becomes familiar place. Abstract space, lacking significance other than strangeness, becomes concrete place, filled with meaning.[16]

Place, in its truest sense, cannot be thrown around as carelessly as our societal norms have unwittingly constructed it. Place allows us to take what is formerly undefined and lacking in significant value and bestow upon it worth through the organization of our emotions and experiences. Place allows us to express deep connectedness to a locale, almost as we would to the people who occupy it. It allows us to experience allegiance and even a diluted form of love for where we are, not just who is present. In other words, what holds my heart in Louisiana and my wife's in California, what contributes to the holiday gymnastics we experience in trying to plan a simple meal, and what causes inter-home wars during football season is this thing we are inextricably tied to—this thing known as *place*.

I am going to great lengths to explain this because this concept must be grasped. Our understanding of place must be central to all our ministry efforts, regardless of urban or rural settings, or something in between. Until we begin to reexperience place within the framework of our theology, and subsequently as an organizing principle of our ministry, then our commitment to seeing "somewhere" change over the long haul diminishes exponentially. This will clearly be difficult, especially in light of Harvey's explanation of our overuse of the idea of *place*. It is mostly lost on our society, and our level of mobility and constant accessibility seem to be the greatest contributors.

To be blunt, place cannot be irrelevant. The idea of moving in and being fully present is not mine, and as much as I like Florida's urging, quoted earlier, to consider thoroughly the relationship between place and our economic future, and our personal happiness, it wasn't his idea either. It's not a new idea, not by a long shot. This belief that place is not only relevant but sacred is seen in the story of Jesus. If we believe that God is who He says He is, then we believe that He is all-powerful, all-knowing, all-everything. This means that God had a myriad of options when He pondered how it was that He'd engage and ultimately rescue creation as a whole and, with specificity, humanity. He could have done some incredible display through nature, like a flood. He could have spoken from the sky or a mountain, as in Moses's case. He could have done anything in any way He desired for His greatest and final effort at engaging His creation so they might turn to Him. And what He decided to do still creates wonder and confusion in my mind—He moved in.

> And the Word became flesh and dwelt among us, and we have seen his glory, glory as of the only Son from the Father, full of grace and truth. (John 1:14)

Jesus's incarnation (God becoming human while remaining God) is the model for ministry. It is at the heart of a theology of place. Jesus came and for thirty years was simply present. He did no miracles. He spoke no recorded words. He taught nothing and did nothing for thirty years except learn the place and culture of the people He'd been sent to serve and save. So what *should* that mean for us?

CALL IT WHAT IT IS

Sin . . . attaches itself to [good] creation like a parasite. Hatred, for example, has no place within God's good creation. . . . Nevertheless, hatred cannot exist without the creational substratum of human emotion and healthy assertiveness. Hatred participates simultaneously in the goodness of creation . . . and in the demonic distortion [fallen-ness]. . . .

The great danger is always to single out some aspect or phenomenon of God's good creation and identify it, rather than the alien intrusion of human apostasy, as the villain. . . .

As far as I can tell, the Bible is unique in its uncompromising rejection of all attempts to . . . identify part of creation as either the villain or the savior. All other religions, philosophies, and worldviews in one way or another fall into the trap of failing to keep creation and fall distinct, and this trap continues to be an ever-present danger for Christian thinking.[17]

Al Wolters's words here are important in helping us transition from ideas to action. They are important in revealing to us the many worldviews that have shaped how we interpret culture, our role in the world, and the Word of God. His words reveal the great danger we are in as Jesus's followers to forget the covenant God made with creation—the one we've toured at length—and the mandate He handed down to humanity to steward it. They remind us, once again, that the material world was made good and was subsequently infected. They inform us of the fact that we should neither idolize nor demonize God's good creation. They are foundational for our understanding that as we wait for God to fully eradicate this world of the fatal infection of sin and fully establish His in-breaking kingdom, we have a present role to play in this renewal and recovery plan.

In having you wrestle with these sometimes polarizing ideas of a holistic redemption, in which all of creation is party, my hope is simple: I hope to inspire you. I hope you leave these few pages with a renewed sense of your ability to influence and shape culture, your ability and calling to renew this world and promote human flourishing for God's glory and the common good. I hope you walk away from this book believing that cultural renewal is not only the responsibility of the Christian but also the most freeing way you can turn your quiet longing into discernible action. What longing? The longing for human flourishing that is present in the heart of most every human being, even if you are not a Christian. It's the reason we feel good when we do good things. It's the longing we sense when we watch late-night infomercials about starving children. It's the longing I sense when I see the same homeless families week in and week out, wondering what exactly I can do so they experience the kingdom of God.

We inherently long for the world, the whole of creation and its people, to function and flourish as they were meant. It's in our DNA. The command to promote and steward creational flourishing was given to Adam and Eve in Genesis 1:28–29, and though they revolted against God's goodness, the command was never rescinded, just recalibrated. Where once their ability to carry out this command was a function of their full and uncorrupted humanity, carrying out the command now necessitates the explicit influence and power of God. Christ came and secured our ability to re-begin the work as intended, by giving Himself over to the justice of God, in our place, and by exchanging our sin-sickness for His righteousness. He gave us the Holy Spirit, and by the Holy Spirit, Christians can reengage in the creation mandate and do so in a way that causes creation to begin to reflect its future reality now. This understanding is in every sense critical to the ministry of presence. It is in every sense the beginnings of a full-scale cultural renewal. Cultural renewal is humanity's present effort at beginning to fulfill our future hope. Cultural renewal is humanity's contribution to the full scope of God's redemptive plan to restore creation and, with it, human flourishing.

CULTURAL RENEWAL

But perhaps when you see the phrase *cultural renewal,* you have no definition for it or way to even conceive what it is. Maybe it's a foreign concept. Here is my attempt at defining it:

> Cultural renewal for the Christian is our interpreting culture through a biblical lens and, through those interpretations, forming a worldview that we then allow to shape everything we do—art, media, leadership, law, music, management, even the mundane—and through these means promote and produce human flourishing and creational order that is a foreshadowing of the world to come.

This is the grand renovation, the redemptive recovery plan, requiring us to leverage every gift we've been given in every sphere we have influence, in every place we are placed, so we can produce, promote, and see a glimpse of the world as God created it to be. God will enact the restoration of His world and, with it, human flourishing. This is the promise of all Scripture. But perhaps one more look at the words of God, through one of His prophets, would be beneficial.

In the book of Amos we have a gloriously aspirational recounting of God's words to His people. The word pictures paint for us a beautiful work of art, and as we gaze at its lines and brush strokes, we are inspired, made hopeful, and believe that our longing for human flourishing will be fulfilled. It is this very inspiration that should generate an unyielding pursuit of the renovation of this present world by God's people while we simultaneously cling to our future hope when, as *The Jesus Storybook Bible* says, "Everything sad will come untrue."[18]

In this section, here's what we need to do. First, we need to look at this beautiful poem and understand what God does and what His people are said to do in concert with Him. Then we need to see some very clear implications and ask some very real questions of ourselves regarding cultural renewal, both as individuals and as the body of Christ.

GOD'S PROMISES

What will God do? That is a fair question. Aside from the *proto-euangelion* in Genesis 3:15, we did not exhaustively cover God's promised restoration of the world. Nor did we explore any of the many biblical images of the world made right or what our home will be like when that work is complete. In Amos we have some incredible pictures of the coming sinless world and all the benefits in store for us. Amos writes that God says,

> "In that day I [God] will raise up
>   the booth of David that is fallen
> and repair its breaches,
>   and raise up its ruins

and rebuild it as in the days of old,
that they may possess the remnant of Edom
and all the nations who are called by my name,"
declares the LORD who does this. (9:11–12)

The day God speaks of is the day when He will come to reclaim what is His, namely, His world and His people. He gives four promises regarding His activity in the coming restoration. God says He will repair, He will raise up, He will rebuild, and He will restore. Each promise is directed to His people and this material world, promising to make it as it should be. The language and ideas in this passage may at first seem foreign to you, but it should for only a moment because we are all well acquainted with the idea of king and kingdom from fairy tales and movies, if from nothing else.

God, in assuring his original listeners of their present/future hope, first begins by reminding them of something about which they would have often reminisced—the era in history when Israel was a great nation under the leadership of King David. In its immediate context this was a promise to God's people that He would one day return them to a state of holistic prosperity, greater even than in the days of King David's rule. God uses the reign of David as a lesser-to-greater comparison to give them an idea of what He is proposing. Though their once-great nation is like a house in ruins, He will rebuild it and rebuild them again. He will repair their breaches, or weak places, and make them able to prosper as He intended. Life will be secure and fruitful again as a direct result of God's actions.

But how do we non-Israelites connect to these promises? We need to go forward for just a moment. In Acts 15:6–21 the leaders of the new church, just established by Jesus, are meeting to decide how they will receive non-Jewish people into their mostly Jewish-Christian churches. There is great debate over several matters, and in the midst of it, James, Jesus's brother, quotes this very passage from Amos 9 in his speech to the other leaders in the early church. He uses God's words through Amos as evidence that the Gentiles (us) must be included and welcomed into the family of God. In Amos's record and James's leverage of it, we see that the narrative of Scripture is holistic in redemption's thrust, material in redemption's scope, and *transcultural* in redemption's outcome as it relates to the redeemed family of God.

TRANSCULTURAL

Transcultural is likely a foreign word to you. It's a word I first applied to the narrative of Scripture and the Christian community nearly half a decade ago. As words go, it is a bit unwieldy because it must capture every nuance represented by the word. But I believe you will grasp it quickly as you see the flow of ideas and the depth of the word's usefulness, particularly as it relates to God's intentions for His world and His people. Here is my definition:

Every human being is endued with the *imago Dei,* the image of God, captured in unique cultural and ethnic expressions which embody the full breadth of God's creative genius, not to be subverted by the ethnic/cultural identity and preferences of another, but celebrated in creating a fuller expression of our humanity, a woven tapestry of color, culture, and class as God forms a people for Himself from all people.

In nearly endless succession, every section of Scripture (Law, Prophets, Poets, and so on) communicates this very idea: God's family can only function correctly in God's world if every people group on the planet is a part of and contributes to the life of His family. In Amos it is no different. God speaks here of all the nations who are called by His name. James, centuries later, uses this very declaration of God to ensure our right to be a part of God's family and party to God's promises to restore His world and, with it, human flourishing.

That is what the Lord says—and that is what He will do. But the promises of prosperity don't end there. This final piece of poetry describes the economic and relational flourishing that will take place in this declared future, founded wholly on the promises of God:

"The days are coming," declares the LORD,
   "when the plowman shall overtake the reaper

and the treader of grapes him who sows the seed;
the mountains shall drip sweet wine,
and all the hills shall flow with it." (Amos 9:13)

God states emphatically, *Look! When I have raised up, rebuilt, repaired, and restored this world—this material world and My people—things will be so abundant that when the harvest comes, those who reap and pick the grain from the fields will still be gathering it in when the one who plows the fields for sowing new seed comes to do so. Look! One day things will be so abundant that the one who treads grapes to make wine will not be finished treading when sowing time arrives again. In fact, there will be so much to make wine with that it will seem as if the mountains themselves are dripping with it.* These agricultural references are important because when Adam and Eve rebelled against God, tried to be God, and invited in this fatal infection of sin, the ground itself was cursed. The land. The materialness of creation itself was cursed. But here God is clear that He will eradicate the infection and reverse the curse! The ultimate idea is that there will be more than enough for God's people. No one will ever lack again. There will be complete economic flourishing.

It is not surprising then that when economic flourishing is inexorable, a stable society is inevitable. God promises in the closing words of this poetic series, "I will restore the fortunes of my people . . . and they [now enjoying full, unfettered humanity] shall rebuild the ruined cities and inhabit them; they shall plant vineyards and drink their wine, and they shall make gardens and eat their fruit" (v. 14). Along with economic flourishing, society will be immovably stable, and there will be relational flourishing and an enjoyment of God's people in light of God's restorative work. God will return His people to a state of prosperity and flourishing.

As an aside, let me say that this is why cities are important, because they aren't ever going away. Can you imagine living in a sinless city? No fear, no crime, no hustle to hoard or gain at any cost. No economic strain or governmental ineptness. Imagine your city, your suburb, your *place,* but fully flourishing and free of sin. This is the future hope God has promised to fulfill.

In their flourishing *they* will plant vineyards and enjoy the wine from those vineyards. *They* will make gardens and enjoy the fruit from those gardens. All in light of the abundance described just moments ago. All in reflection of their societal and relational flourishing. Note the materialness of everything described here. This is not some ethereal cloud existence but an existence that is tangible, made of earth and sky and buildings and people. This is a vision of the future flourishing of God's people when God's restorative work is done. God restores, and His creation, including humanity, thrives.

> Christianity did not come into the world to condemn
> and put under the ban everything which existed before-
> hand and everywhere, but quite the opposite, to purify

from sin everything that was, and thus to cause it to answer again to its own nature and purpose.

—Herman Bavinck, "Common Grace" in *Calvin Theological Journal*

This is yet another question to grapple with as you consider God's plans and promises. Hopefully you're inspired by the future expectation laid out in Amos, but maybe you're lost on how it affects your and my present reality in *this* world. Where do we go from here? What does all of this have to do with cultural renewal?

That Longing

We must acknowledge the concreteness of the longing briefly mentioned just a few pages back. The longing in our hearts—no matter how distinct or diffident—for human flourishing, for a world that functions as it should. It's real. It's tangible. It's identifiable. And according to God, through Amos, it's biblical!

If you have any remaining doubt, there's one place I can quickly point to where this longing certainly rears its head. Just a thought: Why do we get so frustrated with our political leaders? Why are many of us so dependent on them, their policies, and their keeping promises? It's because we want someone to fix what we all know is wrong. We want our leaders to usher in the flourishing that we all desire. And each time one of them fails, we turn and look to others, hoping they will be adequate for the task. But they will never be adequate. Yet during every election cycle we look to them again in hopes that they will "fix America," "fix the economy," "get us to a place of prosperity," and so on. The cycle of longing, hope, and disappointment begins over again, each and every time.

The alternative then is not only to trust the promises of God but to continually acknowledge our longing and know in whom to place our expectation of its fulfillment. The only leader adequate to usher in the future era of holistic healing of God's creation and human flourishing is God Himself. And God Himself has come as that leader, in the flesh, in Jesus. If your hope is not fully in Him, versus the many other people we place our hope in, not only do you not know what to do with your present longing for the flourishing of humanity and healing of this world, but you are in danger of never knowing a world without brokenness or a life full with hope.

Jesus is humanity's great leader, and He must be trusted as such. If we trust Him, we must also trust His words. It was He who said repeatedly that the kingdom is here. It has broken in. The future reality of restored creation and human flourishing is upon us. It has been purchased in the righteous sacrifice of the God-man, Jesus. He gave His life in exchange for the horror that is the darkest parts of our individual and collective souls. For these reasons, then, we cannot limit redemption to the justification of the individual soul. I repeat, we cannot limit redemption in that way. Redemption applies to the whole of creation, because our great leader says it does. God reconciles all things, including this material world, to Himself in Jesus (Colossians 1:20).

ALL THINGS MEANS ALL THINGS

The "all things," the materialness of this reconciliation provided by Jesus is proven, not only in His incarnation and subsequent sacrificial death, but in His physical, fleshly resurrection. This is vitally important. As much as Jesus's followers love to, rightly, dwell on the cross, we seem to miss the significance of the resurrection. The physical resurrection. Without the resurrection, the cross is nothing more than the place that a kind, miraculous, Jewish carpenter died after promising His band of followers, and any who would give Him an honest hearing, that He was, in fact, God. But we know Jesus was more than we can fathom, more than a kindhearted Jewish carpenter, and so we must put equal emphasis on the resurrection, what it meant, and the key it is to understanding the renovation of the material world.

Jesus, in His incarnation, was the "fullness of God" (Colossians 1:19). Yet when He rose from death, He rose with a body, a physical body. His disciple Thomas even poked at the holes in His hands because they were hands of glorified flesh (John 20:27). The resurrection is proof that God made both the spiritual and material world and that Jesus returned from the spiritual to the material world. His resurrection points to the redemption of every part of this material world, promising that it, too, will one day be glorified. One day He will return again to claim what is His. This is the full scope of the gospel. This is the full scope of God's redemptive and restorative work. The Holy Spirit regenerates the human heart and restores the face of the earth. It is both. And it is beautiful.

Putting Away a Childish Thing

Let's say you have acknowledged your longing and your need for a leader to fulfill that longing. (Perhaps you haven't. Give it time!) It is necessary to also acknowledge that though much work has been done to prove the biblical grounding of this idea—God's total restorative work in creation and our present participation in it—for many this is antithetical to what we were taught.

Most of us grew up in Christian dualism. (Dualism being a philosophical term defined as the division of something conceptually into two opposed or contrasted aspects, or the state of being so divided.) I'm about to drop two names here that (a) you probably don't care that much about or (b) you may not even know. And that's fine. But I need to give credit where it is due, so bear with me. Lesslie Newbigin, the great missionary and thinker of the twentieth century, pointed out that Immanuel Kant's (one of the most influential philosophers in the history of Western philosophy) concept of a bifurcated reality is the essence of the modern world. It's the late-enlightenment-period idea that drives our current perspective that my life as a Christian and my life as a person are somehow distinct and divided.

Dualism, applied to modern evangelicalism, creates two vacuums. In one is my personhood, everything in my day-to-day reality that makes me, me. In the other is my faith, and that faith is tied to specific times, places, events, and "spiritual" contexts. They (my faith and my life) do not overlap in any significant way in the broader aspects of what makes up my world. Dualism makes it impossible for us to have a comprehensive biblical worldview, because it separates the spiritually sacred from all other aspects of life.

> There are not sacred and profane things, places, and
> moments. There are only sacred and *desecrated* things,
> places, and moments—and it is *we alone* who desecrate
> them by our blindness and lack of reverence.
> —Richard Rohr, *Eager to Love*

Dualism allows us to look at our faith in private, individualistic, self-focused terms and eliminates the possibility that faith can be macro in scope. Or that the gospel can have far-reaching, social implications. Since my faith and my life are divided, then what I do for work or what I create with respect to art or music or how I engage in culture is distinct and has little bearing on how I live out my faith. Inversely, then, my faith has no bearing on how I shape or renew culture.

This way of thinking, this worldview, has created a host of

issues in the church, and I believe it is the primary contributor to the impotence of the church and its inability to truly change the neighborhoods where it gathers, least of all the world.

Further, dualism leaves most of Jesus's followers with a belief that the only way to serve God is through vocational ministry—teaching, preaching, missions, and so on. If not vocational ministry, our faith is limited to serving on Saturday evening or Sunday or in a community group setting (our church, Renovation, calls these City Groups), and that being the extent of the arenas where faith, or at least its outworkings, is exercised.

Christianity then becomes a means of personal peace, forgiveness, breakthrough, and strength, but not an interpretation of the world around us. In reality, dualism is little more than a Christianized form of Gnosticism, which says that the spiritual world is good and separate from the material world, which is "bad" or at least "not spiritual." Within this framework, the Christian looks to his or her faith for a personal spiritual life, but the dominant voices in culture interpret everything else for them. This leads to a debilitated view on how we change culture, and from that debilitated view we automatically turn back to one (or more) of the four established ways that most Christians believe we change culture.

THE POWER TEAM!

The first way in which Christian dualism leaves us helpless to try to change culture is through the salvific intent of the gospel alone, meaning many believe that cultural renewal will happen purely through evangelism. In other words, if enough people get saved, then culture itself will shift. I'm all too familiar with this established way of thought. I was, for a short time, a member of the Power Team. If you are unfamiliar, Google it, but leave off my name—please!

The Power Team was a group of strong-man preachers who would travel the country and host "evangelistic crusades." During these crusades we would perform "feats of strength" (Festivus anyone?), including but not limited to rolling frying pans into burrito-like shapes, bending one-inch rebar, popping soda cans, ripping phone books and license plates in half with our bare hands, breaking massive stacks of concrete blocks (often on fire) with our forearms, and my personal favorite, running full speed through a pair of two-by-fours taped together—also lit on fire. We would attribute each act and our ability to do it to the power of God. After the "show," we'd give a strong (and regrettably sometimes less-than-biblical) evangelistic appeal for any in the audience to be saved. We truly believed we were reshaping culture and righting the world through our efforts. But how far could the impact of it and other similar event-centered, evangelistic efforts really go? Yeah, not very.

Though evangelism is good and right, it cannot and will not single-handedly renovate our culture. And if we believe that pursuing the salvific intent of the gospel is the sole means we have to transform culture, then we limit redemption to the justification of a single soul. And this we've already seen massively truncates the effects of Jesus's righteous death.

If every part of God's world is broken by sin, then the goal of redemption—the restoration of God's ruling power—must be the renewing of every part of creation. Lives, relationships, neighborhoods, and everyday aspects of being human are healed and rewoven with one another to the degree that they come under the authority of Jesus. This is why what God says in Amos is so tangible, societal, and material. Everything must be made new, not just individual, sinful souls (see Psalm 72; Isaiah 11:1–10; Colossians 1:16–20; and Ephesians 1:9–10).

Listen to David's words in Psalm 72:

> May his name endure forever,
>> his fame continue as long as the sun!
> May people be blessed in him,
>> all nations call him blessed!
>
> Blessed be the LORD, the God of Israel,
>> who alone does wondrous things.
> Blessed be his glorious name forever;
>> may the whole earth be filled with his glory!
> Amen and Amen! (verses 17–19).

Redemption will ultimately entail the complete healing of creation, the "whole earth" being filled with the glory of God. This cuts across social justice, the reunification of all humanity, and the end of all physical decay and death. Knowing this, we work to bring the health and coherence of Christ's lordship back into every aspect of human life, not just to evangelize those who have yet to experience Christ's salvific work. The church is supposed to be a new humanity (see Colossians 3:1–11) in which the world can see what family life, business practices, race relations, neighboring, and all of life can be like if God's world was as God intended, right now.

ALL FORM BUT NO POWER

I say this about evangelism knowing that the overreaction to an evangelistic view of cultural change is equally popular, particularly among Millennials. If dualism doesn't trap us in an evangelistic box, an oftentimes gospel-less or gospel-light form of social justice is ready to receive us. The new urban renewal movement is filled with well-intentioned people who truly believe in abiding by the heavily misquoted words of Francis of Assisi: "Preach the gospel at all times, and if necessary use words." Okay, here's the deal—no source before 1990 records that he ever said these words, yet I have heard them on a monthly basis over the last six years. They have been used to undergird a belief that doing good for good's sake is doing the work of God. The problem with this belief is that it in no way distinguishes our work from the work of, say, the atheist. As a side note, one of my best friends in Atlanta is an atheist, and I'd put his work done and dollars spent on improving our city up against any Christian. And I believe he'd win or be a close second.

What separates our good works from the good works of those who aren't in the family of God is the motive behind our efforts. The motive must be the gospel and its far-reaching effects on the world as it is, and its healing attributes, which will make the world be as it should. The motive must be the creational covenant that God made with all things He created and our call to steward His rule in the world. The motive must be our desire to create change in our cities, our towns, and our places that foreshadows the kingdom to come. If our motives are less than that, we cannot count our work as contributing to the renovation God is enacting in His world.

Give Us a King

If evangelistic fervor à la the Power Team or doing good solely for good's sake doesn't become the lens through which we see an opportunity to change the world, then change through political action is somewhere many people easily turn. The general idea is that culture can be changed through politics and politicians. The limitation with this view is what we've already discussed—we live in constant frustration with our political leaders because they cannot do, to the full extent, what we long for them to do. Why, then, would we put our hope in politicians and politics? But we do, whether Republican or Democrat.

Here's what I mean. During the 2012 presidential election, I was coerced into a robust political conversation, the details of which I will spare you. The other person was intensely vested in the idea that every Christian should vote for Mitt Romney. When I asked why, after unwillingly entering this conversation, I was told that Romney, though a Mormon, shared "our values," the "our" being those of evangelical Christians. There are varying issues with this ideology, but the foundational issue is the belief that if we can somehow elect enough Christians, pseudo-Christians, or "moral" cult participants to office, then they will change culture by legislating Christian, or otherwise moral, values.

First, this essentially amounts to having a theocracy. Second, this would directly grate against the mandate that every one of Jesus's followers has been handed; namely, to be missionaries to those who are not a part of the family of God and to renew our culture through the means He has given us in the spheres He has placed them. Third, it's simply lazy, unengaged faith that would desire so uninvolved a solution as simply electing officials to govern the choices of people by legislatively binding them to the biblical narrative.

This does not mean we don't participate in the process. But it does mean that filling the government with Christians, or with people who supposedly espouse Christian values, is not the ultimate answer. We should want godly people to run for office and figure out how to apply a biblical worldview to their office, but only to the extent that it is where God placed them to serve Him and see culture renewed.

GRRREAT!

The final means by which most Christians believe culture will change is what Dr. Timothy Keller calls "the Great Person

Approach."[19] In other words, Christians are always waiting for the next singular figure who will write books, make speeches, write music, and create art—and through this one individual, culture will shift.

Lecrae Moore happens to be a part of the Renovation Church community. He and his family are faithful participants in the life of our church. Because of his recent musical success, there is much talk, even some around Renovation, about Lecrae single-handedly changing culture. This is a false construct, and he would be the first to tell you so. It is also an example of extreme historical amnesia. His desire is to be faithful in his sphere of influence and for other followers of Jesus to do the same so we can renew culture together. Culture is changed through community, not heroic individuals. Renovation happens through networks of people who think critically about culture and seek out ways in which the gospel can be applied to their work or creativity, creatively.

Yet we are constantly waiting for the next Martin Luther or Martin Luther King Jr. or Abraham Lincoln. But this is faulty, because faith is not individual but communal. God consistently speaks of a collective people, not individuals. And our efforts to renovate our culture must be seen in the same light.

THIS IS WHAT WE DO

So here's the call. In other words, this is what we do right now.

Believe That God Delights in the Material World He Has Made

> The eyes of all look to you,
>> and you give them their food in due season.
> You open your hand;
>> you satisfy the desire of every living thing.
> The LORD is righteous in all his ways
>> and kind in all his works. (Psalm 145:15–17)

This psalm is an extrapolation of the doctrine of creation and reflective of God's covenant with all of creation. If the material matters to God, it should matter to us. If God satisfies "the desire of every living thing," then those things should matter to us. We cannot see culture renewed if we believe culture and the material world to be something separate from the work of God or His intentions in this world.

Hold Fast to the Fact That God Has Made a Promise and He Plans to Keep It

If God is going to keep His promise, should we not live in light of that? This means that we must remind ourselves often, maybe daily, that this world is God's prized possession. And if He says that He will bring it back to flourishing, then we should dig in and begin to see that flourishing take shape wherever He has us, through whatever means He's given us, until He comes to consummate it all.

Pray! Pray for Renewal in the Places God Has Placed You and in the World at Large

When Dr. John Perkins and I were doing a conference together, he said to me, "Renewal is connected to prayer." As we act, we must pray. We are literally praying for the renewal of all things (Matthew 19:28, NRSV). If you believe God intends to renew this world, pray about what part He intends for you to play. Pray that He gives you eyes to see the work He has for you to do. Pray for your neighbors, neighborhoods, and political leaders. Pray that He comes quickly to fulfill His promise.

Bring a Holistic Biblical Worldview into Everything You Do, from the Magnificent to the Mundane

One way to begin to do this is to ask good questions of yourself with respect to wherever God has you in life right now. For example,

- How does a Christian do business? Would you make less money to have more impact in renewing culture and the world? Example: Chick-fil-A will put a store in an underresourced community and will not close that store even if it does not turn a profit, because they know the store brings jobs to and uplifts the community.
- How does a Christian create art? Example: Can you interpret culture through your art form and then tell a better narrative based on your biblical

worldview? Denzel Washington famously stated that his character in *Training Day* had to die because "the wages of sin is death." He rewrote the ending of his character specifically to showcase his biblical worldview.

- How does a Christian engage politically? Example: Pray for your leaders. Vote issues instead of the party line. Don't get co-opted by a certain group because of rhetoric or tradition. Work on a campaign to help a godly individual get elected who has a plan to renew culture and better your community. Work with groups like Street Grace—an organization that lobbies for laws to protect women and end child sex trafficking.

- How does a Christian choose a home or neighborhood to live in? Is it driven by fear, safety, comfort, or something greater? Example: Choose a home in a community that needs stable families or economic uplift and begin forming community there. Invite other Christians to move in with you for the express purpose of renewing a neighborhood. This is intentional neighboring, and it is antithetical to the American Dream. This fights against the American economy of isolation, the system in which we primarily exist that tells us to isolate for our good in the safest place we can find.

These are just a few examples of a nearly endless list. The driving question is how will your biblical worldview influence every decision you make, promotion you take, school you choose, or art you create? How will you, with what you do, promote human flourishing and reflect the world to come, the world described by God in Amos? Those are the things we must keep in view in order to truly renew culture.

Plant Your Life in a Place and Rebuild What Is Broken by the Means God Has Given You to Promote Human Flourishing in Every Respect

We live in one of the most transient eras in history. There can be no substantial influence or change in any place if our goal is only to be there long enough to get what we need from a place and then move on. Renewal is only sustainable if you commit long term to a place and a people. Transience generally only serves our own ends, but planting our lives in a place for the good of it serves the ends of God.

Live Interconnectedly and See All of Humanity That Way

Quite simply, you can't live life unaffected by what happens in some other part of the country or world. And you can't live life alone. Life is meant to be lived in community. God is returning for a community. God made us to feel connected to one another in a way that leads to empathy and sorrow when we see suffering, no matter how far from us it occurs, and celebration and joy when we see good, no matter how far from us it rises.

What Does Flourishing Look Like?

We've seen glimpses of it. Movements and events like the Great Awakening, the civil rights movement, the end of apartheid, and William Wilberforce's (and his community of cohorts through their political power) tireless battle to end the slave trade in Britain. These efforts were driven to one degree or another by the biblical worldview of communities and by the networks of individuals who felt the strong call of cultural renewal. They followed that call, and culture changed and flourished.

God made us to delight in His world, and if it hadn't been for the fatal infection of sin, we would have gone on delighting in His world, making music, creating art, doing business, or whatever God has gifted us to do. It is because Christians believe in a coming age without sin and injustice that they eagerly work in this world to bring about foreshadows of the world to come. This belief should influence everything we do. By making this world flourish, otherwise known as being a great place to live, which is what God intended, we are doing the work and will of God.

I'll close this section with this quote by Mark Noll:

> Who, after all, made the world of nature, and then
> made possible the development of sciences through
> which we find out more about nature? Who formed the
> universe of human interactions, and so provided the raw
> material of politics, economics, sociology, and history?

Who is the source of harmony, form, and narrative pattern, and so lies behind all artistic and literary possibilities? Who created the human mind in such a way that it could grasp the realities of nature, of human interactions, of beauty, and so made possible the theories on such matters by philosophers and psychologists? . . . Who, moment by moment, maintains the connections between what is in our minds and what is in the world beyond our minds? The answer in every case is the same. God did it, and God does it.[20]

———

Consider your context, where you are right now. Now think back about the four ways most Christians believe culture is changed. Which one is the most predominant in your context (and this may include the context of your mind)?

_____

_____

_____

_____

_____

_____

Five

The Sanity of Sentness

Here I am! Send me.

—Isaiah 6:8

One of the most vivid memories I have from recent years is also one of the lowest moments of our time in Atlanta. January 14, 2009, was a critical juncture in the life of what would become Renovation Church, because that was the winter day our Jesus-centered, socially conscious, transcultural movement almost never came to be. Why? Because I was finished. Actually, I was done. No más.

I alluded to these things earlier, but it's worth mentioning in detail that at this point in our efforts in Atlanta, I'd been beaten down by countless calamities and could see no hope for our future in the city. That morning I sat at my makeshift Ikea desk, staring out at the snow-covered parking lot of our loft and feeling the weight of all the previous months' difficulties press against me: my inability to find a job for nearly six months, running out of money and having to pawn or sell most of our possessions, having various utilities shut off at one point or another, our first ministry team suddenly falling apart, plus my general inability to gain any traction in the neighborhood or execute the extensive plan I'd put together to see change come about in our neighborhood. In my mind, I'd failed and failed miserably. The only solution I could imagine at the moment was to pack up my family and get out of there.

No Idea

Breanna and I moved to Atlanta knowing there were problematic aspects, but we had no idea that the night we moved in someone would be murdered across the street from our loft. We had no idea that every single day we'd see the same sunken faces up and down Memorial Drive looking for food or money or both. We had no idea we would come to know so many children who were one crisis away from being a statistic. We had no idea that the first funeral our church would be involved in would be that of a ten-year-old boy. We really had no idea.

When we first broke the news to our parents that we were moving to the inner city of Atlanta for the sake of seeing the community change, both sides reacted with equal parts shock and fear.

"What about your daughter? Where will she go to school?"

"Will you guys be safe? Crime there is outrageous."

"Why can't you live somewhere else and just drive in to help?"

Those were fair questions, and to some degree they were right. Crime here is above average. In fact, three of the twenty-five most dangerous neighborhoods in America (two in the top ten) are within a mile of our neighborhood. Some of the locals, particularly Christians, were no different than our parents.

"Why would you want to live down there with those people?"

That was the impression many had and continue to have. The city is a place to be feared. A place to drive by on the interstate. A place to avoid unless absolutely necessary. But never, and I mean never, a place to move in and raise a family. I must admit on that winter day of my discontent, I started to believe they were right. I started to dwell on the intense sadness I saw in the faces of the homeless men who sat outside our building every day. I started to shudder at the thought of something happening to my wife or daughter. I started to create scenarios in which we became a crime statistic. I started to believe, if for just a moment, that the city could not change, that it is indeed a place to escape from.

While this is not a book about my wife, I must say this: Breanna is amazing. In that low-point moment, she placed her hand gently on my shoulder and reminded me that what we were doing was much bigger than us. She firmly told me that the sacrifices we'd made were not in vain. She assured me she was with me, thick or thin. She encouraged me by saying she still believed in a better Atlanta and, for whatever reason, we'd been invited to be a part of that dream becoming a reality. She told me we were staying, no matter what, and she challenged me to see the city with fresh eyes.

From that day forward, I never saw the city in the same way again. I realized we had gotten only half of the equation correct—we'd moved in. The second half of our equation, the half we'd gotten wrong, was that we had moved in with a grand plan to "save the city." But we did not truly know the people or the place; in other words, our plan was premature. You cannot have a plan for a people you do not know. I have revisited these words countless times over the last few years.

What we needed was time and the ability to see the city through the eyes of the people who were already here. I don't want to overplay that day, but it truly was an awakening as I then saw our "failures" as gifts in disguise, for they forced us to toss out our own plan and truly become a man and a family and a church of our context, our place—Atlanta. The place we were sent.

SENTNESS

What if we chose the place we live because we had a sense of *sentness,* a sense of calling? What if we chose a place based not on how it would serve our ultimate happiness or economic future or delusions of safety, but rather on how it would serve to cultivate in us a revolutionary understanding of why we are on this planet in the first place? What if we lived with a genuine theology of place, a belief that God is intricately involved in and interested in all the details of our lives, right down to the zip code we call home?

In an incredible declaration, the church planter/missionary/apostle Paul confirms just that. Dr. Luke tells us that Paul, in a speech to the philosophers of Athens, shouted with persuasive authority:

> The God who made the world and everything in it,
> he who is Lord of heaven and earth, does not live in
> shrines made by human hands, nor is he served by
> human hands, as though he needed anything, since
> he himself gives to all mortals life and breath and all
> things. From one ancestor he made all nations to
> inhabit the whole earth, and he allotted the times of
> their existence and the boundaries of the places where
> they would live, so that they would search for God and
> perhaps grope for him and find him—though indeed
> he is not far from each one of us. For "In him we live
> and move and have our being." (Acts 17:24–28, NRSV)

God made everything. God is involved in everything. God is interested in everything that happens in the world He created, including where you live. Why? First, so that you "would search for God . . . and find him." But second, so you would be a means for others to do the same. What does this mean for us? This means that choosing a place to live must involve ascertaining first if God has determined for us to be there. Are we truly sent? Do you feel sent by God to the place where you currently live or are you just in the most convenient situation available? Do you feel as though your life is lived with a God-given vision for your community because He has you there for a reason? Or was the neighborhood "nice" and the schools "good," and it felt "safe," "advantageous," "artistic," or . . . ? You fill in the blank.

Have you limited yourself in such a way that your sense of place is determined by how you can best be served? It's a legitimate question, especially in light of the prevailing cultural view that where I land is primarily determined by the opportunity it affords me. Could it be, though, that God is calling us to something greater? Could it be that God, who determines the boundaries of the places we live, is calling us to the places where there is little opportunity for us but massive opportunity for others through us? Could it be that you are far more valuable to the mission of God than you have ever imagined? Could where you live and why you live there be a function of His redemptive work in the world?

The Stanleys

I first met the Stanleys, a family in our church that lives in Adair Park, because Becca, a wife and mother of four, found my blog. She saw a post I'd written about planting in the city, and she reached out to me about our families having dinner some evening. We had them over to the old loft, and though we talked for hours about many things, what struck me most that night was her statement: "We feel that God is sending us to the city, so we are selling our home in the suburbs. We just feel sent here by Him." I will never forget that conversation or their resolve in submitting to God's sending so they could be exactly where God wanted them to be. The Stanleys were willing to give their lives to the well-being of the city.

It has been stunning to watch the continued growth of their investment in their neighborhood over the last several years. As much as I would love to paint every experience as though it has been an energy-filled, conviction-led, smooth ascent of their walking in this calling, I cannot. Even a sense of sentness can be challenged by the costs associated with being fully present in difficult places.

To that point, where the Stanleys live is within blocks of the Blue Store, an icon of the community known for a concentration of gang activity, though it is nothing more than a local convenience store. It's not uncommon for the Stanleys to regularly hear gunfire, or in worst-case scenarios, see the evidence of it in their front yard. Since the Stanleys have two young children under the age of six, this creates seismic tension when living in light of, and within proximity of, these realities. There are more stories and internal struggles than I have pages or permission to share. It's not just the external factors that weigh on the Stanleys but the internal as well. As though the environment itself was not wrought with enough challenges, their work with the teens they call their extended family can be equally tumultuous.

Recently, two of the young men with whom the Stanleys have worked the longest—both in their day-to-day tutoring and home-based relational ministry as well as in their well-attended extended-stay summer camps—have suddenly pulled away. They began by verbally challenging the validity of their relationship, the depth of their investment, and the purity of the love the Stanleys have for them. They stopped coming by for dinner, refused to answer their phones, and all but cut them off completely. One of these young men ended up committing a crime that left him facing time in a juvenile detention facility, angry now at the Stanleys for not finding a way to bail him out of his bad decisions. And yet, in all of this, I have not seen them shrink back. Hurt? Yes. Cry? Sometimes. Feel overwhelmed and want to walk away? Certainly. *But their sense of sentness will not relent* and will not allow them to do anything less than be all in for the well-being of our city.

If this radical transformation can happen in their hearts, then wherever you are in your understanding of place, it too can be altered in a moment. This means that you could, today, see your neighborhood through new eyes, see your city or town through a carefully cultivated sense of place. Nothing must remain the same. When your heart gets turned inside out, and

God begins to awaken in you the idea of your sentness, a theology of place begins to take root in your soul. In this moment, the possibility for change is limitless. Here are a few questions to ponder:

- Are you where God would have you to be?
- Do you see yourself as sent to your community?
- Do you have a theology of place, an understanding of your responsibility, an ownership of every issue that plagues your community?
- Do you feel the weight and passion that surround a God-given vision for immeasurable change?

I hope so, because God would have no less.

If you are willing, truly willing, then the opportunity that lies in front of you to see your city or place become what God intended is not a pipe dream; it is an achievable reality. But first you must determine if the place you're in is the place He'd have you, and if you're willing to give your life to its well-being. Don't miss that last phrase—*willing to give your life to its well-being.* Yes, this will involve sacrifice, the root of which, interestingly, is "to make sacred."

GENTRIFICATION?

Of course, there is another way to see a community change that doesn't take into account God's intentions to restore His world, the scope of the gospel and all its implications, or the sacrifice of actually being sent, no matter the place or cost. It particularly affects the urban landscape, is rarely talked about, and unfortunately is both purposefully and incidentally embraced by the church.

Imagine for a moment that you've lived in the same home for two decades. It is not an extravagant home, but it is *your* home. Through sheer willpower, luck, and stringing together multiple jobs, you've made ends meet. You've even raised children in this home. You've endured economic downturns, the rising and falling and rising of violent crime and drug distribution, failing school systems, and lack of access to basic things like banks and grocery stores. But relatively speaking, you're settled in life and its offerings.

One Saturday afternoon a moving truck pulls up to the house next door. You've wondered what was going on over there. There was an industrial Dumpster out front for the last month or so, and you've seen more people coming and going than you'd seen on the block in years. The house hadn't been lived in for the last five years, so you think it'll be nice to have new neighbors.

A young couple pulls up in a nice car. To your surprise they're . . . white. *White folks haven't lived down here since the late sixties,* you think. But you're not a racist, so it doesn't really matter to you what race your neighbors are; it is just notable that they are young and white.

Months come and go and life progresses as usual, except you continue to see more and more new faces in the neighborhood. *Mostly* young. *Mostly* white. It also feels like every home in the neighborhood is getting a facelift of some sort: new roof, second story, additional rooms, landscaping. You think, *It's nice to see people take pride in this place again.*

As the holidays draw near, you prepare to welcome family, have big meals and loud, boisterous conversations. And as it is every year toward the end of the year, you get your property tax bill. But this year's has doubled from the previous year. You've never been poor in the conventional sense of the word, but you have just barely made it by and even managed to save a little. But this? How can you contend with this? Soon you're forced to make a critical decision: lose your home for failure to pay taxes or sell your home and move. Either way, you'll be starting over. Either way, you will be displaced.

This hypothetical scenario illustrates the "gentler" side of gentrification. Describing gentrification is often easier than defining it, as there are nuances, layers, and complexities to how it happens, to whom, and how it is perceived. But there are shared ideas across the spectrum of definitions:

> The process of renewal and rebuilding accompanying the influx of middle-class or affluent people into deteriorating areas that often displaces poorer residents. (*Merriam-Webster's Collegiate Dictionary*)

> The buying and renovation of houses and stores in deteriorated urban neighborhoods by upper- or middle-income

families or individuals, thus improving property values but often displacing low-income families and small businesses. (Dictionary.com)

When "urban renewal" of lower class neighbourhoods with condos attracts yuppie tenants, driving up rents and driving out long time, lower income residents. It often begins with influxes of local artists looking for a cheap place to live, giving the neighbourhood a bohemian flair. This hip reputation attracts yuppies who want to live in such an atmosphere, driving out the lower income artists and lower income residents, often ethnic/racial minorities, changing the social character of the neighbourhood. It also involves the "yuppification" of local businesses; shops catering to yuppie tastes like sushi restaurants, Starbucks, etc. . . . come to replace local businesses displaced by higher rents. (UrbanDictionary.com)

Sociologist Ruth Glass coined the term in 1964:

One by one, many of the working class quarters of London have been invaded by the middle classes— upper and lower—shabby modest mews and cottages— two rooms up and two down—have been taken over when their leases expired, and have become elegant,

> expensive residences. . . . Once this process of 'gentrifi-
> cation' starts in a district it goes on rapidly until all or
> most of the original working class occupiers are dis-
> placed and the whole social character of the district is
> changed.[21]

Gentrification, in short, is the rapid multiplication of the wealthy and equally rapid evacuation of the indigenous and often-poor population of a place. As innocuous as we may perceive this process to be from where we sit, it is far from it. In imagining yourself on the receiving end of even the "gentle" side of gentrification, I hope you can see that though the American Dream drives so much of what we do and the choices we make, many people lack just that, choice, and so they are subject to the outcomes of our capitalizing on our capitalistic system.

To be clear, I stress this form described above as gentle because a more aggressive form does indeed exist, where ambitious and wealthy individuals con, persuade, and—in the case of many elderly residents—deceive people into selling their homes to them. They in turn invest modestly in renovating those homes and then sell them for up to five times what they invested in them. They do this rapidly, and some investors can own an entire street of homes and/or businesses, using them as money-making machines while having little regard for the current or former residents. In most cases this is legal. But is it ethical? Or if I may ask in a more penetrating fashion, is it redemptive? Is there an alternative in which we, as Jesus's people, should view this differently and thereby *do* things differently? The answer is unequivocally yes. We live sent lives and "seek the welfare of city" (more on that in a moment) rather than our own welfare, and in doing so we create a culture of dignity for those to whom we are sent.

I have certainly not always done well in helping to create a culture of dignity, particularly as the pastor of Renovation Church. In fact, and without intention, our church began to contribute to what we'll call, forsaking argument, the problem of gentrification. When we realized what we'd done, it was almost too late.

Prior to the launch of Renovation and well into its first two years, I led us to a distinctly city-centric, almost neighborhood-centric model. We didn't want anyone driving in from the suburbs or beyond to be a part of our community, and we had great reasons for that focus. Atlanta's growth in nearly every respect (as we've already discussed), including church life, had been toward the suburbs for decades. First Baptist of Atlanta was likely the last influential church to flee the city, and with it and many others gone, the gospel movement languished in Atlanta. When Breanna and I moved in, in 2008, we found fewer than ten churches that were preaching the gospel and living on mission in the intown neighborhoods. It was simultaneously exciting and disheartening. Of course, with seven years behind us now, we can rejoice that there are several great gospel works that have sprung up in the city, and it seems there are many more on the horizon.

For these reasons, and a belief in proximity to community, we were stern in our position. It was not uncommon for me and other leaders to send people away, asking that they find a community near their home in the suburbs. It was not uncommon for us to even post a list of churches that people could go to, instead of making the drive all the way to ours. These hard boundaries pushed many families to make a significant decision—should they move into the city in order to partici- pate in the life of our church? They did so by the hundreds. It was quite stunning to see so many people willingly sell their homes or allow their leases to expire in the suburbs so they could move in, rather than drive in, and we celebrated it—but there was an unforeseen cost. What we were doing, uncon- sciously, was nearly gentrifying entire neighborhoods, particu- larly in our most underresourced parish on the southwest side of downtown. I'd inspired, through proclaiming the gospel and calling people to seek the welfare of the city, hundreds of people, mostly white, to move into mostly minority and eco- nomically depressed areas. Our church was gentrifying! I was heartbroken. I felt shame even though it'd never been the in- tent. We knew we had to do something, but what?

After recognizing what was happening, we did something that you may find radical, dictatorial, or overreaching—we put a moratorium on moving into certain neighborhoods. You might be thinking, *That sounds insane!* In some ways it was, but we understood what was at stake. We knew that we could not sit idly by, preaching a gospel that considers the ethical implications of every decision and seeks the welfare of the city, while undermining those very words with our actions. Of course, the only leverage we had in this scenario was influence through relationship and leadership, but we leveraged all we could, where we could. We sought to stem the tide, and for the most part, it worked.

For the many who had already moved in, we provided resources, training, and hours of conversations to help shape their posture in their neighborhood and equip them to be good neighbors. Under the leadership of one of our parish elders, a late-fifties retired missionary, and also white, these singles and couples who'd made the move into this particular area of town began to work diligently at becoming indigenous in every sense. They invited their neighbors into their lives and were subsequently invited into the lives of their neighbors. Some of the stories that have surfaced from this are priceless, including the gifting of nicknames that several have received from their new friends. They have organized strategic conversations about fighting gentrification in their neighborhood and helping to create opportunity for their neighbors who don't have the means or access to create it for themselves. They have taken a subordinate position to their indigenous neighbors' desires for the shape of the neighborhood, and they have used their energy and resources to make the neighborhood a great place for every person there rather than used it to try to reshape it in a way that will only benefit them. It is really quite beautiful. They have, by God's grace, gone a long way to create a culture of dignity rather than succumb to, or even celebrate, the gentrifying wave that has hurt so many neighborhoods and will hurt so many more. They have taken God's side, related to the disenfranchised, lived sent lives, sought the welfare of their community over and above their own, and make no mistake, it has often been both complicated and costly.

Riley in the SWATS (Southwest Atlanta Too Strong)

Living sent lives is both complicated and costly, as we've noted. There are many stories I'd be honored to tell, but there's at least one that can be told by the man who lived it. Below is an e-mail I received that accurately captures the potential tensions that arise when you seek to live redemptively and sent, creating a culture of dignity rather than flowing with the tide of self-serving intentions.

PL,

I hope this e-mail finds you well. It is Riley Brookings sending this from good old Capitol View.

I have an issue that came up with two of my neighbors that has created a lot of tension and stress around C View. I talked to Christie and Brian Holben, and they recommended I e-mail you.

My neighbor right next to me is a paranoid white guy that is extremely "law abiding" and prosecutes anyone to the full extent of the law when (he deems it) necessary. Our friendship has grown over the year, and we have had some very heated discussions on faith. We are swapping books back and forth because we both love philosophy. His wife and he have both been a part of our lives over the year, and we are their only friends. They look down on the prostitutes and "sketchy" people in this neighborhood, and they really trust no one.

Last week I was dragged into civil court in regard to a feud he and my [other] neighbor are having. It has to do with an alleyway, but the situation has risen to the point where they take each other to court over dumb things like loose dogs [and] grass clippings dumped into the alleyway, etc.

Long story, but I had to testify that I witnessed a conversation and no one hit each other. It was horrible, and after the court appearance, my neighbor was very upset. He can't stand this neighborhood and how people break the law. He will continue to uphold the law to the full extent. He then warned me about the handymen I use.

I use two old black men that are rough guys. Both

men have committed petty crimes in front of him, disposing grass clippings illegally. Never have these men done that while working for me. Both of these handymen are my friends. One is a brother in Christ. My neighbor told me if these men commit a crime while under my hire, he will prosecute me along with them. I am still using the handymen, and he is totally upset with that. He can't imagine why I would be so ignorant.

Sorry it's so long, that is some of the context. I want to continue to have a friendship with him, but I really want to avoid him because of his attitude toward my friends. Any thoughts or advice on what to do? I am thinking a difficult conversation might need to happen, and I am willing.

Thanks for your time in reading this.

Much love,

Riley Brookings

Riley's desire to love all of his neighbors has created incredibly difficult circumstances for him. One of his neighbors, the "paranoid white guy," desires that the neighborhood be rid of the indigenous neighbors. This Riley shared with me in a subsequent meeting after I received his e-mail. This particular neighbor despises those who resided in the neighborhood before he moved there, and it is his intent, through the reporting and prosecution of petty crimes—that is, dumping grass clippings—to get them to leave or get them arrested so they are taken away. In fact, he communicated to Riley that his intent was to "turn over" the neighborhood. Does this feel redemptive?

This is the uglier side of gentrification in an individualistic expression. When it becomes corporate, the pace and damage leaves entire neighborhoods gutted of the cultural, ethnic, and economic diversity that so characterizes the kingdom of God. It leaves entire neighborhoods gutted of the cultural, ethnic, and economic diversity that should characterize our churches as well.

TECHNICALLY, YES. CONVENTIONALLY, MAYBE . . .

This wave of gentrification is not limited to any one neighborhood or even city. This is important to note, because if you took the time to look, I imagine you'd find that this issue is affecting your city, your place, in less than redemptive ways. Perhaps more than you presently want to admit.

For example, I went to Seattle recently. As I spent time visiting friends, I had an interesting conversation with one of them, Mike Anderson. We were talking about crime, impoverished neighborhoods, and the gospel. We were discussing the gospel's reach, societal implications, and what, exactly, we should be doing. He then told me about the "ghetto" in Seattle, an area called White Center (no less), and some other areas that are considered "rough." You may notice that I have placed both *ghetto* and *rough* in quotations. I've done that to show the sarcasm that must be captured, because what I discovered in these areas led me to conclude that if these were the rough areas of Seattle, then Seattle truly had no 'hood.

Generally, in true 'hood areas, there are things you find and things you don't. Banks, grocery stores, coffee shops, sushi bars, Target, Barnes & Noble, and so on are not to be found in depressed communities. Why? Because these businesses generally know they cannot be profitable in depressed areas. It's why, even now, though my neighborhood is mostly gentrified, we still can't get Whole Foods to come in. What you do find in depressed areas of metropolitan cities are liquor stores, pawn shops, corner stores (that charge eighty cents for one pack of Kool-Aid, true story), burned-out or abandoned buildings, and masses of people standing on street corners. The "rough" areas of Seattle had all of the former and none of the latter. It is probably the clearest picture of the quiet effects of gentrification as well as a clear view into the fact that for the most part it goes unnoticed by us.

The effects of this wave of gentrification are also important to note, because whether you know it or not, it is affecting your ministry, as a pastor or simply as a person, in profound ways.

As young professionals, artists, and hipsters (of which I've been called) are moving back into cities, and as gentrification imposes its will on once-depressed areas, there is an adverse effect that is easy to miss if you're not being attentive to the change. Here in Atlanta we have seen sometimes light, sometimes severe, but always present, culture clash. What Riley described earlier is a heartbreaking, but often more benign form of this. But in more extreme examples, it can be far worse.

Case in point: I live in Grant Park (downtown Atlanta), one of Atlanta's oldest and most historic neighborhoods. Our home is near Martin Luther King Jr. Boulevard, and everyone I know who doesn't live here or isn't familiar with what has taken place here always asks me, "You living in the 'hood now?" Well, technically yes, but conventionally no. We've lived in several different places in this neighborhood, including in what was once an abandoned warehouse turned chic, overpriced loft spaces with gated parking. So more directly, though others might fear this as the 'hood, by all accounts I am living in what is considered a mostly gentrified neighborhood. And it is diverse by race, ethnicity, culture, and class. It amazes me when I see BMWs, Bentleys, and other high-priced vehicles drive past homeless guys urinating in the street, and yet I see it every day. This overlap creates a culture clash that plays out in everything from conversations about education reform to how we should structure the neighborhood association, and it is starting to spill over in more severe ways.

The shopping center where we do all of our grocery shopping is about three miles from my home. There is a Target, Barnes & Noble, Kroger, Best Buy, Lowe's, Ru San's (sushi), Chase (bank), and a Smoothie King, not to mention several upscale shoe stores, shops, and boutiques. It possesses all of the qualities of the "rough" areas of Seattle, so by my general definition, it is no longer a depressed area. Except in Atlanta's situation, because of the pace of gentrification and trend changes, my definition is blown. Why? The liquor store three blocks from this shopping center was robbed, and the clerk was shot to death in the process. Mere weeks after that incident, a shootout between two vehicles occurred in the shopping center housing Target, just a few hours after my family and I finished buying groceries there.

Gated Communities with Invisible Walls

The point to this discourse is to make plain that the dividing lines between rich and poor, safe and dangerous, 'hood and hip are no longer so clear. This is a changing landscape that as a pastor to this city, I am going to have to carefully examine to understand so that Renovation can most effectively and faithfully engage and reach this entire area—that does not in any way lend itself to homogeneous ministry. If we're going to be true to engaging the whole of the community, we cannot allow this to simply *be*.

This is a changing landscape that as a person, pastor, or ministry leader of any kind, you, too, will have to carefully examine, and in the process of examination, wrestle with all of its implications so that you, too, can be faithful to reach your whole community with the whole gospel.

Unfortunately, the church often finds itself in one of two

positions related to this quandary. Either the church is on its heels in these matters, virtually unaware of the implications of the rapid changes taking place around it, or it is unable to change in a timely manner in order to meet the rising demands. Or, and most dishearteningly, the church is welcoming the changes, even celebrating them, as it postures some churches to more easily facilitate ministry to a segment of people and a portion of a place, because that people and that place provide a homogeny with which they are comfortable. A homogeny that we are taught in seminary is both right and necessary to build a healthy church.

It is easy and seemingly prevalent for churches who settle into gentrified or gentrifying areas to find themselves welcoming the wave. In turn they become gated communities with invisible walls, subtly hostile to the other cultures, ethnicities, and peoples around them, those to whom they haven't chosen to minister. These walls are sociological, preferential, linguistic, and class oriented; racial, cultural, and even educational. And this choice, regardless of how we justify it by baptizing it in missional language, lacks the same redemptive energy as many of the gentry themselves.

How then do we do this rightly? How do we diligently work to reconcile the culture clashes? The simple answer is to believe a gospel with enough breadth to call people into the family God is forming for Himself. But fleshing out the specifics of that ideological and theological answer is far more cumbersome. Regardless of its difficulty, for anyone seeking to move into and work for the welfare of any major city, any place at all for that matter, these questions must be answered. And though I don't have all the answers, I do believe that a step in the right direction is to look into the wealth of words that is the book of Jeremiah.

JEREMIAH 29 CHURCH

The church—God's people—reflects the fulfillment of God's promise now, as we seek to see renewal happen in our cities and communities. You may have heard of the Acts 29 Network. I am a part of that organization—a group of churches committed to being a diverse global network of church-planting churches. But what if I challenged you to become a Jeremiah 29 church? Would you have the slightest idea what I was talking about? Here are the first seven verses in that pivotal chapter:

> These are the words of the letter that Jeremiah the prophet sent from Jerusalem to the surviving elders of the exiles, and to the priests, the prophets, and all the people, whom Nebuchadnezzar had taken into exile from Jerusalem to Babylon. This was after King Jeconiah and the queen mother, the eunuchs, the officials of Judah and Jerusalem, the craftsmen, and the metal workers had departed from Jerusalem. The letter was sent by the hand of Elasah the son of Shaphan and Gemariah the son of Hilkiah, whom Zedekiah king of Judah sent to Babylon to Nebuchadnezzar king

of Babylon. It said: "Thus says the LORD of hosts, the
God of Israel, to all the exiles whom I have *sent* into
exile from Jerusalem to Babylon: Build houses and
live in them; plant gardens and eat their produce.
Take wives and have sons and daughters; take wives
for your sons, and give your daughters in marriage,
that they may bear sons and daughters; multiply there,
and do not decrease. But seek the welfare of the city
where I have *sent* you into exile, and pray to the LORD
on its behalf, for in its welfare you will find your
welfare.

This is an incredible framework for what it looks like when
God's people, believing in their sentness, work for the good of
their city, their place. Though the Israelites were exiled far from
home, God commissioned them to be reflections of His promise, to be good neighbors, to be those who sought the welfare of
their community. Like the people of God exiled in Old Testament Babylon, the church lives as those set apart for God's service, not only for themselves but for the whole of the city. In
these ways, then, we seek to answer those questions. In these
ways, we seek the renewal of our city.

SEEING YOU ARE SENT

First, we understand that we are sent. I've already mentioned
this, but sentness is central to our identity as followers of Jesus.

In Jeremiah 29:4 we read, "Thus says the LORD of hosts, the God of Israel, to all the exiles whom I have sent into exile from Jerusalem to Babylon." How did God's people end up in Babylon? God sent them there. In the same way that God sent His people in the Old Testament into Babylon, if you are a Christian, you were sent into your city or town or neighborhood. If God sent you, you are exactly where God wants you to be. *You are sent.* You don't simply exist in your neighborhood, in your county, in your city. This means that every moment happens with intentionality. God sent you to reflect His glory and establish His good in renewing that place, not only spiritually, but culturally and physically as well.

This is the reason our City Groups—Renovation Church's small-group communities—are geographically based. The goal of a City Group is to live sent lives together, not simply have Bible studies or be with the people we get along with best. Each City Group owns the spiritual apathy or confusion, physical brokenness, needs, pains, hurts, struggles, and fears of the community in which it exists. City Groups are the primary way Renovation Church loves and serves Atlanta in God's renovation of the city. Your understanding of sentness will determine where you spend your time, what eateries you frequent, where you work out, the stores where you do your shopping, and all of the various things we do day-to-day, described as normal life. These decisions become intentional if you see yourself as sent by God in seeking renewal where you are.

GROW ROOTS

In addition to seeing ourselves as sent, we are to establish permanence and invest in infrastructure. God says through Jeremiah, "Build houses and live in them; plant gardens and eat their produce" (29:5). Transience is one issue most churches, and unfortunately all urban churches, deal with. Young urban dwellers are notorious for not putting down roots. This is proven in the job market, where people now have some twenty-plus jobs by the time they're thirty. This is proven by rental occupancy rates that turn over, on average, every couple of years. This is even proven by worship attendance, which is now counted as "regular" if it is twice per month. Generation Xers and Millennials are quite possibly the most transient generations to ever live. No place feels this more than cities. Most people who live in the city do so when they are young, and then they move out when they have children or when seeking a better school system or a larger home.

Yet God calls His people to live differently. Through the voice of Jeremiah, He calls them to build homes and "live in them." What He is communicating is that this is no short-term stop or event-based service opportunity. This is a long-term investment in renewal, one that requires you and me to grow roots. I (mostly) appreciate the heart behind the efforts of those who don't live in the city but want to serve it. But it does not help the homeless child or the heartbroken prostitute for someone to drive from the suburbs or beyond, give them a meal or a new set of clothing, a prayer (maybe), and then drive away. Those things either perpetuate their brokenness or fail to move them toward a fruitful, productive, Spirit-led life.

TRESTLETREE

If you were to ask me what solidified this shift in my thinking and gave legs to this ideology of presence, place, and sentness, I could easily capture it in one word—Trestletree. Trestletree is a small Section-8 housing community that exists in my neighborhood, Grant Park. Trestletree has been here for the better part of thirty years, and though the neighborhood has changed around it and in most cases become hostile toward it and the people who live there, God used Trestletree and the people who call it home to fundamentally alter me and the face of our ministry.

After the three false starts we had in trying to get Renovation Church off the ground, I began to rethink everything. Everything was on the table, including my not-so-brilliant plan to rescue Atlanta from itself. We went back to the foundation. No plan, just prayer. On one of our weekly prayer walks around the neighborhood, my small team and I encountered a group of women sitting on the steps of one of their units. They looked . . . ghostly. I froze as I took them in with my eyes, unable to move, unable to speak. The Holy Spirit moved my heart in that moment, and I was sure that I was to go over and pray for them. Though I was filled with a strange fear, I obeyed His prompting and I approached. "This will sound strange," I said, "but I feel I am supposed to pray for you. How can I pray for you?" Addiction. A job. My children. These, among other things, were the requests made. They did not rebuff me. They did not seem put off in any way. The sense of the Spirit's presence in that moment was palpable. From that day forward, nothing would be the same.

After the prayer, I asked them if there was any way we could serve them. Note that I asked them; I did not propose a solution or an ideal for their lives.

In order to understand how a community will receive the gospel, how a community can experience renewal, it is best to ask those who were there before you rather than assume what they or the community as a whole needs. Not every depressed neighborhood needs a new coffee shop.

Their response seemed simple enough: "Please do something for our children." We took them seriously and began to pray and devise ways we could serve them and their children. Being an ex-professional athlete, a day camp that incorporated sports and an opportunity to hear about Jesus over a meal seemed like a perfect answer. At this inaugural camp we had some fifty children, and technically we weren't even a church yet! We would repeat this effort for a few years, and each time the attendance increased and the impact was greater. The camp effort led to community cookouts and concerts (at Trestletree), tutoring, weekly pickup of up to forty children (once we did start worship gatherings), and even a Renovation-sponsored soccer team.

All of this happened because we didn't have a plan, but rather we were good neighbors, present among the people to whom God sent us. And we were sensitive to the Spirit, which made us willing to do whatever He asked in order to serve the vulnerable and see the community change. Of course this was not without its difficulties. In an effort to do some asset-based community development, we started a cleaning service. This decision was based on the desires of some of our single mothers. For various reasons it failed, but we had no regrets in trying. Without question though, the most difficult situation of all was the untimely death of one of our Trestletree children. He was only ten. I still have a picture of us playing flag football together at our very first camp.

I did not imagine, when accepting this call, that the first funeral I'd ever do would be that of a ten-year-old boy, but those are the realities that come with dwelling faithfully among those to whom God sent us, especially in this type of neighborhood. Because we had become family, we were able to endure the difficulties. Because we were among and not above, we were able not only to minister but also to be ministered to by them.

God's people need to live among their neighbors, for that's where real renovation happens.

When we build houses and improve the neighborhood by being good neighbors and good stewards of our things, God is renewing through us. Permanence, not transience, is how God renews. Interestingly, some research shows that ownership even creates an affection for your neighborhood and an emotional connection to the place and the people. I know I feel it. Many who have put down roots in the city will tell you the same thing. Building a house means you can't just pick up and leave. You are locked into a community. The question for every Christian who hopes to be present, to minister from a sense of presence is: Are you connected or making plans to be? Are you praying about moving into the neighborhoods of the city you feel called to reach so God can reflect and renew through you and among those who live there?

NOT JUST A JOB

In this view of renovation, we are not only called to build houses and live in them, we also need to invest in the infrastructure of the city. How? By producing goods and services that not only meet our needs but ultimately serve those around us. The Israelites were an agrarian society. This means their economic system in large part was based on farming, their ability to work and cultivate the land. What they produced through this cultivation was a contribution to the overall well-being of the city of Babylon. Okay, but how does this translate? We renew by contributing to the common good of our cities through our work. I'm not the first person to say this by any means, but I'm continually surprised at how many people have never thought about their work in this way. Your job is not just a job. It's an opportunity to be used by God in your vocation to contribute to the overarching good and overall infrastructure of your city or place. This is not simply a matter of the will, though. This is the result of a heart transformed by the gospel. What Jesus accomplished on the cross—dying in our place for our self-serving, self-worshiping nature—should extend into every aspect of our lives. If He is not the means and motivation, then it ceases to be a gospel work. This position of ministering from presence transforms work from being an often soul-sucking means of only providing for ourselves into a life-giving means of communicating the hope we have in Jesus and creating ways to contribute to the common good of the city.

My friend Travis Vaughn, a geographer, urban student, professor, and well-known writer, shared this with me:

> Cultural renewal is about recovering the biblical pur-
> poses of calling and vocation . . . so that our life and
> work glorifies God, integrates our God-given gifts,
> desires, and abilities, and serves the common good in
> the places God sends us.

How we work is a reflection of who we serve. This is why, motivated by the gospel and empowered by the Spirit, Christians must strive to be amazing employees. God is making our towns and cities better by cultivating and creating through our work. Renewal happens when we understand we are sent, establish permanence, invest in infrastructure, and plan for a long and faithful work.

IT TAKES A GENERATION OR TWO—MAYBE THREE

God says in verse 6 of Jeremiah 29, "Take wives and have sons and daughters; take wives for your sons, and give your daughters in marriage, that they may bear sons and daughters; multiply there, and do not decrease." This may not seem immediately applicable to the modern believer, but take a moment and look at the principles distilled here. Do you see how many generations were just listed? At minimum, God has an expectation on Israel that they are there for three generations. You read that correctly—three generations. This idea of taking wives, giving our children in marriage, and their having children has far-reaching implications for renewal in the places we find ourselves sent by God.

First, it means that if God has called you to see renewal happen, you should reconcile with yourself that this is no overnight job. Renovation Church has the privilege of being present in what is happening in the lives of children and families in a few Atlanta neighborhoods like Grant Park and Summerhill and Adair Park. We are also involved in midtown with the realities of homelessness and sex trafficking and in Akers Mill with tutoring and mentoring. Rest assured, these are not one-year, five-year, or even ten-year works. What we hope to see may not happen in our lifetimes or possibly even in our children's. What you hope to see will likely be the same. We work, we invest, we pray, and we plan so that what we begin is carried on by them. Are you in it for the long haul? Do you need to see immediate results, or are you willing to walk and work by faith, knowing that the work is ultimately the Lord's, knowing He will carry it on long after you are gone?

WE ARE FAMILY

The second thing we must not miss from this verse is the idea of intermarriage, although not specifically in a racial sense. What God is telling His people is that they are to become family with those who are already in the city or place where He's sent them. They are to welcome them into the family of God. This is crucial. This means that we are not better than those we seek to serve and assist in renewal. We are not better. We do not treat people as projects to be fixed but as those we are folding into the family of God. Further, if people in your city or town come into the family of God, no matter their educational or economic background, no matter their racial or ethnic makeup, we should be willing to consider them among any other as marriage material for ourselves if we are single and for our children if we are not. Again, this is crucial, and I admit radical. But such thinking is vital for the kind of renovation God desires.

In these ways—living out our sentness by establishing permanence, investing in infrastructure, and planning for a long and faithful work—we seek the welfare of the city or place where God has sent us. Plus we pray on its behalf, for in its welfare we find our welfare. Are you poised to seek the welfare of your city, meaning its greater good? Do you want your community to be a great one, reflecting the glory of God who created it? If your answer is yes, then you must pray for your city. Prayer is spiritual breathing.

Prayer is not passive. It is active in its power as we plead with God to *move*. Prayer, not a plan, led us to the incredible opportunity we've had with Trestletree and many others. Ask the Holy Spirit to burden your heart to pray for your place. Ask the Holy Spirit to break your heart for what breaks His. Ask the Holy Spirit to bring you to tears over the exploitation of children and the hurt of the fatherless. Ask the Holy Spirit to make you restless over the institutions that uphold poverty and racism. Ask the Holy Spirit to give you a supernatural love for your neighbors. Ask Him to drive you to your knees in prayer for legislators, in prayer for city government, in prayer for the school system, in prayer for the hurting, the hopeless, and the lost. Ask Him to hold your heart fast to His as you seek to see renewal happen. Ask Him for His help in praying on behalf of your city, your county, and your neighborhood where He's sent you. Ask for His help in seeking the welfare of your place, because as your place goes, so will you. You are tied to your community's economic, social, and cultural well-being. How you engage that truth will determine your ability to be effective.

As the City Goes

If the schools are bad, it affects you as well. If medical care in the area is poor, it affects you as well. If neighborhoods are dangerous, it affects you as well. The list could go on. Here is something vital to remember: whatever plagues the city will ultimately plague you. The alternative is what has already taken place with the church in previous generations. The church had no theology of place, decided its welfare was not tied to the cities, and it left. Will that be you? I pray not. I pray yours will be a community that seeks the good of your city.

> Three critical factors have determined the overall health of cities—the sacredness of place, the ability to provide security and project power, and last, the animating role of commerce. Where these factors are present, urban culture flourishes. When these elements weaken, cities dissipate and eventually recede out of history.
>
> —Joel Kotkin, *The City: A Global History*

Kotkin, in speaking of the "sacredness of place," is directly referring to religious institutions. He is by no means a Christian, and yet he sees the vital role the church and, in his estimation, other religious institutions play in the health and welfare of our cities. How could we not see the biblical, vital role the community of Christ has in seeking the good of our cities when someone from the outside looking in can? We must renovate.

We must be diligent in seeing our cities and towns reflect the city to come. This means that the community of Christ creates and cultivates goods that help, even enable the cities where they reside to look more like God's great city in every way possible. This is not a work of the will but the outworking of a heart that has been transformed by the good news that Jesus came, died, and was resurrected for His glory and our good, extending His righteousness to those who put their trust in Him.

Renewal in all facets of the social structure of a place is an implication of the gospel, as the gospel has a deep, vital, and healthy impact on business, the arts, government, media, and academia of any society. Doing good from any motive other than living out of who Jesus is and what He's accomplished will eventually lose its luster and have little lasting impact. It is those things we do when motivated by Jesus that have eternal weight. We work for renewal as an outworking of Jesus's finished work in us, not in an effort to earn His approval or that of anyone watching. Every one of us, from academics to artists, in every aspect of our work, must understand why we ought to create or cultivate cultural good.

We need to dream again of what our cities and towns and neighborhoods would be like if God's reign was tangible and His good was extended in such miraculous ways that they began to reflect His glory. We need to dream again of what it would look like for the church to flood the neighborhoods that no one wants to live in and no one talks about, giving their lives away in those communities for the sake of the gospel and the good of the city. God wants more for my city, your city, and every city, town, suburb, village, and place of this world. He wants what He once called good to be restored, renewed, and renovated so that it can reflect His perfect glory. That future hope begins here and now with us.

Can you see glimpses of a Jeremiah 29 church in your current faith community? If so, what's the strongest piece of that picture? What would be the most challenging aspect of such an approach?

And if not, what in the world are you and your church doing?

_____

_____

_____

_____

_____

_____

_____

_____

_____

Six

The New Reality

If we don't come together right now on this hallowed ground, we too will be destroyed, just like they were. I don't care if you like each other or not, but you will respect each other. And maybe . . . I don't know, maybe we'll learn to play this game like men.

—Coach Herman Boone, *Remember the Titans*

The celebration from the crowd was palpable. The unthinkable had just occurred. After a perfect season, not losing a single game, T. C. Williams High School, an integrated and diverse school, had just won a state title, and Denzel Washington's swagger never looked better. Most of us are familiar with the movie *Remember the Titans,* but because it is a movie, we can regrettably forget that it was a story based on the lives of real people.

In 1971, though still dealing with racial unrest, the city of Alexandria, Virginia, decided it was time to totally integrate their school system. A step toward this goal involved hiring an African American coach, Herman Boone. We have to keep in mind that the US Supreme Court actually mandated desegregation in 1955, so the fact that it took Alexandria sixteen years to follow through on this tells us a great deal about the state of racial tension there.

The movie gives the true account of white players who refused to play with their black teammates or for their black coach. In the same way, the story line shows black players who refused to play with their white teammates or for white coach Bill Yoast. While the school was integrated on the surface, it was not in their hearts. And unfortunately, in every sphere of life, from the schools we attend, to the neighborhoods we live in, to the places we work and even worship, this is still a looming reality: we are integrated on the surface but still segregated in our hearts. In the community of Christ, this is simply not acceptable.

If we are to strive for more than merely filling a room with people who have vast differences, we must fill our *lives* with people who have little in common with us other than the cross. This is the call God has placed on those He has rescued and invited to His table. The gospel, by design, moves us beyond integration and into true community. Concerning this, Paul writes to the Galatian church:

But when Cephas [the apostle Peter] came to Antioch,
I opposed him to his face, because he stood condemned.
For before certain men came from James, he was eating
with the Gentiles; but when they came he drew back
and separated himself, fearing the circumcision party.
(Galatians 2:11–12)

Now, in order to understand what's going on here, it's imperative to have some understanding of what came prior to this moment; in other words, context.

THE FOLKS OF CHRIST

The book of Acts is basically the record of how things went down in the forming of the early church. Among other things, we are told that Stephen was murdered for preaching the gospel (Acts 7), and the new church in the city of Jerusalem began to be persecuted. Because of this heated persecution, many of Jesus's followers were literally run out of town under the threat of death. One of the places they were scattered to was the city of Antioch, a large melting pot of a city situated as the geographical and political crossroads of east and west in the Roman Empire.

Men of Cyprus and Cyrene [came] to Antioch [and]
spoke to the [Greek-speaking non-Jews there] . . . ,
preaching the Lord Jesus. And the hand of the Lord

was with them, and a great number who believed turned
to the Lord. . . . And in Antioch the disciples were first
called Christians. (Acts 11:20–21, 26)

Out of this scattering and subsequent preaching of the gospel was birthed a beautiful and diverse church, a place where
both Jew and Gentile were not only coming to faith in Jesus but
now worked, worshiped, and walked together in community. A
new reality had come into being with this community whose
identity and self-definition centered neither on their Jewishness
nor their Gentileness but rather in their collective devotion to
the One in whose name they shared a common life.

Thus they were called *Christianoi*—the folks of Christ.
While the term *Christian* has taken on many different conno-
tations today, in Antioch it meant one thing: those who follow
Christ and live according to His teachings. Christians then
were not only those who loved God, but those who also sought
to love one another in community. Only the Prince of Peace
could unite people so different, creating a family out of people
from every tribe, nation, and tongue.

Even the leadership at Antioch was diverse. According to
Acts 13, there were in the church prophets and teachers—
"Barnabas, Simeon who was called Niger, Lucius of Cyrene,
Manaen a lifelong friend of Herod the tetrarch, and Saul" (verse
1). It is worth noting that Luke takes the time to list these men
not only by name but by ethnicity as well. Could it really be a

coincidence that two of these men were from Africa, one from the Mediterranean, one from the Middle East, and one from Asia Minor? I don't think so. God was making the point that His people would include all people, not just in surface-level integration, but in the deepest possible levels of relationship and leadership in His church. Why was that contextual clue important? Hang on.

WHAT GOD HAD IN MIND

Many Jews thought that in this new way of following Jesus, Gentiles needed to essentially become Jewish first. This is what some Jews had in mind, but it was not what God had in mind. In Antioch, He was fulfilling His promise to bless all nations by drawing some from all nations into His family. No one knew this better than Peter. He'd been joyfully sharing meals with non-Jewish Christians, experiencing the freedom of the gospel as a Jew crossing the ethnic barrier to eat with Gentiles. There was nothing staged or artificial about this. They were natural relationships, eating with one another, just kickin' it. And it was good. But suddenly, when other Jewish Christians showed up, Peter segregated himself by only eating with other Jewish Christians. In addition, the Scriptures indicate that Peter not only stopped eating with Gentile believers, but eventually he stopped associating with them altogether. And Paul says that because of this, Peter was out of step with the what? The gospel, and he stood condemned.

It's probably wise to pause a moment and pinpoint the reason behind Peter's behavior. Scripture is quite clear: Peter was afraid. He was fearful of what the Jewish Christians would think or do when they saw him sharing not only meals but life with the Gentile believers. And because of his position of influence, Peter's fear infected the other Jewish Christians at Antioch, resulting in a complete withdrawal from the community of Gentiles.

> And the rest of the Jews acted hypocritically along
> with him, so that *even Barnabas* was led astray by
> their hypocrisy. (Galatians 2:13)

Even Barnabas? It was at this point that Paul had had enough and confronted Peter publicly, face to face. In that verse from Galatians, the words *hypocritically* and *hypocrisy* literally mean "playacting" and "crooked walking." Paul is not mincing words here. Peter's integration was surface only. His heart was woefully divided. Racism or classism of any kind in any culture is incompatible with the truth of the gospel. And anyone who denies this truth stands in opposition to the new creation God is bringing into being.

I remember being the only African American elder at a former church post and feeling the withdrawal from a couple of the other elders when racist church members would come around. In fact, one of the men asked me if I was always going to have that "rapper hair." Evidently one of his friends in the church had complained about it. Yeah, about my hair.

NEW ETHNICS

One of the central outworkings of the gospel is the breaking down of ethnic, economic, and cultural hostilities and building up of communities that capture the full breadth of God's creative genius.

> For he himself is our peace, who has made us both one
> and has broken down in his flesh the dividing wall of
> hostility. (Ephesians 2:14)

Jesus broke down these divisions in His own body, securing our salvation and submitting our tendency to separate ourselves to the pain of the cross and the power of His resurrection. Faith alone unites us to Christ. We cast ourselves completely on Him and His righteousness. And for His sake alone, God counts us righteous and accepts and welcomes us into His family forever. This is the heart of the gospel. This is the good news!

In Christ there is a new humanity, a new community, where our identity is defined by the calling of the cross. In Christ the ruling paradigm is that there is no separation; we must, in fact, move beyond integration. And if you think for a second this means we should all just become the same, think again. This is not some attempt at assimilation or manufactured community.

The gospel unites us in Christ despite our differences. In fact, the gospel drives us to celebrate our differences as the diversity-strewn beauty from the Lord's creative hand. And if that is true, then what distinction can we make? Who are our people, our kind? How can we be united in Christ but divided in His family? Living that way would be a *mockery* of the gospel.

As a giant of his time, a native son of Atlanta and a gifted orator, Dr. King has had a profound effect on me. He was by no means perfect, but point me to the man who is and I'll tell you what he's hiding. Dr. King had a dream of a world where race, color, creed, ethnicity, socioeconomic status, and education were not used to generate class distinctions and hostility but rather used to create a woven work of "all God's children" living in love and unity in the beloved community. This should be the dream of the church, because it was greater than simply being a man's vision for the world. It is a dream that is reflective of the heart of God, the dream of His Scriptures, and made possible only by the sacrifice of Jesus.

ALL MEANS ALL

We love our city because we see the potential that we have, through the working of the Holy Spirit and by the power of the gospel, to see this gospel dream become a reality. We love our city because every day we have the opportunity to live out the words upon which our country was founded. On July 4, 1776, our forefathers ratified these words: "We hold these truths to be

self-evident, that all men are created equal, that they are en-
dowed by their Creator with certain unalienable Rights, that
among these are Life, Liberty and the pursuit of Happiness."

These words, penned by the men that founded our nation,
are powerfully wonderful words, but then, as in the minds of
some people now, they were not applied to all whom God created. By 1776 the Africans who'd been shipped to North America as property had been enslaved for almost two hundred years.
Though some thought slavery was wrong, the majority of people saw it as acceptable. Slaves usually could not marry, have a
family, testify in court, or legally own property. Where were
their unalienable rights and equality? And even before the African was shipped to America, the Native American was used as
forced labor. The details of that season of our nation's history
are different, but the result was the same—inequality.

It would be almost one hundred years after those words
were penned in 1776 that slavery would officially end. But
even after this, there was still no sense that all men were created
equal. On the heels of slavery would be another hundred years
of oppression—Jim Crow, segregation, and separate but equal.
Then there were the *onlys*—white-only water fountains, white-
only swimming pools, white-only restaurants, white-only
schools. My own mother, who is very fair-skinned because her
grandmother was half-white due to the rape of her mother by
a slave master, was told by a white teacher that she should
"pass." My mother was encouraged to leave her family and live

as a white woman so she could be more accepted and live an easier life. Equality on the surface does not necessitate equality in our hearts.

STILL THE SAME

I realize that in discussions like this, some will respond, "Yes, but that was so long ago, and things are different now." Unfortunately, things haven't changed as rapidly or broadly as we might imagine. A few months ago I was returning home from one of our worship gatherings in Grant Park, and I saw a man running around my neighborhood and waving a Confederate flag. He was shouting, "The South shall rise again!" I'm afraid the sin and evil of racism and classism has not ended; it has just been governed and suppressed. The words this nation was founded upon are impotent in the face of blatant hatred and systematic division of people along racial, ethnic, social, and socioeconomic lines.

This is the history and, in some places, the present reality of our nation. But what about the church? The visible bride of Christ is supposed to be different, a living example to the world of how humans should relate to God and in turn how humanity should relate to one another. "If then you have been raised with Christ," then by all accounts you should be daily putting off the old self with its practices (Colossians 3:1). Why? So you can live and love well in the new community of Christ, having put on the new self. This is then your primary identifier; it is the way people know you above all else.

The new self is not just a new nature or even a new person. *It is a new humanity altogether.* In this new reality, the forefathers' words can finally become true. This equality across all lines is a re-creation of what was always intended, how human relationships were always meant to be. We all stand equal at the foot of the cross, because we all belong to Christ.

> The renewal refers not simply to an individual change of character but also to a corporate recreation of humanity in the creator's image.
>
> —Peter Thomas O'Brien, *Colossians, Philemon*

This re-creation involves what community was always supposed to be, and this is what it means to be a *New Ethnic.* This term came to me as I was preparing to see our church planted in Atlanta. As I wrote out the mission statement and wrestled with the Scriptures about who I'd like this church to be, this term surfaced.

> We become New Ethnics when we come to follow Jesus and are transformed by the gospel. We are striving to be freed from the bounds of prejudice, fear, and hang-ups of simply being identified by our race, class, or culture. We long to become a new people altogether, a beautiful tapestry of God's creation, called and chosen by Him for something bigger than ourselves. As such, we are deeply committed to being intentionally transcultural.

Audacious, huh? And I say that because if you look at the atrocities of the past, and even those of the present when it comes to racism and classism, you know those attitudes and ideas still exist in the church as well.

Dr. King famously said that Sunday morning is the most segregated hour of the week. For years this is just the way it was. Racial, ethnic, and social divisions existing even in the body of Christ. This inspired the writings of men like Lemuel Haynes, an African freedman, pastor, Puritan, and Republican abolitionist who pastored an all-white church in the 1700s. "No one can, Haynes insisted, be denied freedom or 'Communion' because of race, appearance. ... At 'the comeing of Christ,' Haynes insisted, 'when the Sun of riteousness arose this wall of partition was Broken Down.'"[22] What Haynes means here is that every Christian is equal. Every Christian is family.

CHRIST IS ALL

Here there is not Greek and Jew, circumcised and uncircumcised, barbarian, Scythian, slave, free; but Christ is all, and in all. (Colossians 3:11)

You are likely familiar with these words of Paul, but I'd like to briefly unpack them for the sake of our conversation. These three categories he mentions are very clearly measuring sticks "out there"; in other words, societally. But not "in here"—not in the unfolding kingdom of God where those who have been raised with Christ are being transformed by the renewing of their hearts and minds. Paul outlines three human distinctions with which we are all familiar, but he casts them in different language.

1. Ethnic identity—"Greek and Jew"
2. Faith heritage—"circumcised and uncircumcised"
3. Class, culture, and social standing—"barbarian, Scythian, slave, free"

These were rigid dividing lines, particularly in the first century. To some degree, though in modified language, they are still at play today in our broader culture. But they cannot coexist with the gospel as we routinely conceive them. And so you might wonder, *Then what do we do with our obvious differences. Are we no longer to acknowledge them?* No. It is not that these distinctions disappear, but that they are mediated through our primary identity—we are Christ's and He is everything. Jesus is all and in all.

THE STRUGGLE IS REAL

It'd be easy for me to tell you that I had a gospel epiphany and never had an issue with race or culture or anything ever again. That'd quite simply be a lie. I grew up in southern Louisiana, and next to Mississippi, it might have been one of the most racially tense states in the nation. I have early memories of being called "nigger" at one of Dad's work parties by one of his employee's sons. I remember having it yelled from the stands when I was playing pee-wee football. And I remember walking down the street and having a dip bottle chucked at me from the window of a truck outfitted with a Rebel flag. Experiences like these made me so hateful toward white people that by the time I was fifteen, my own mother, who grew up during the civil rights movement and lived her entire life being discriminated against, called me prejudiced and said, "You are becoming exactly what you despise."

It was in that same year, just before I turned sixteen, that I met Judah Vedros. This kid shared the gospel with me no less than ten times. His persistence finally paid off, and I agreed to attend a youth group service with him. It was at that gathering God saved me. After all the years of bitterness, God sent a young white kid who heavily favored Tom Cruise to show me the beauty of the new humanity. I naively believed I was healed of my prejudice, but there were remnants of that former life that continued to influence my thinking.

Throughout college I toyed with the idea of an interracial relationship but decided to date only inside my race. I partied hard and hung out with a lot of girls during my nearly two-year full-sprint rebellion away from God. But after God reoriented my life, I went on a dating hiatus. During that time I made a list of thirty-seven things (I'm ridiculous) I wanted in a wife; number thirty-seven being that I wanted her to be a beautiful black woman. And then I met Breanna.

The night I met her I went home and told my old man, "I may have met the girl I'm going to marry." Breanna was (and is) beautiful, smart, and musically gifted, and she loved God more than anything. But it wasn't long, even in light of Breanna's overwhelming beauty, before I began to have doubts. She was (and is) beautiful, but she is not black. I didn't know if she would ever be able to fully understand me, and if God blessed us with children, I believed they would go through hell growing up in the South.

But as I began to go through my list, I realized that Breanna embodied thirty-six of the thirty-seven things I desired in a wife. I told my mom about my conundrum, and I'll never forget what she said: "Well, when you begin to trust Jesus, I guess that last thing won't really matter, will it?" And with that statement I was forced to reconcile my theology with my heart. Was I just playing on the surface or did I truly have a heart for what God wanted?

Now, after nearly a decade of marriage, I cannot imagine my life with anyone else. Every time I see my three beautiful children, I am reminded of the power of the gospel. And my heart is filled with joy. After all of my hurt, anger, and reactionary sinful prejudice, God continues to renovate me through my own marriage and family, and to show me what it means to live out the new humanity—to live as New Ethnics. Together, as a family, we have the privilege of leading Renovation Church—a three-times-failed church plant, which is now a diverse and dynamic community of over one thousand people—to do the same. Not for the sake of the church alone, but for the sake of the city, for the love of our place, for the belief that we can see substantive change, and with the understanding that we are working out God's desires, however imperfectly, every step of the way.

THE MINISTRY OF PRESENCE

Right now, in this moment, you are in a dangerous position. Why do I say that? Because if you've read this entire book, you did not heed my warning at the beginning to return this book immediately and try to get your money back. Or you really do want your life, your family, your church, your *place* to change. And you *believe*, through the power of God's Spirit and at least some (hopefully all) of the principles in this book, you can see and be a part of that change. If the latter, wonderful! But I stand by my words. You are in a dangerous position all the more. Why? We've turned over some big rocks in this work. We've laid a theological foundation for why this present world matters to God and, subsequently, why it should matter to us as we seek to renew culture. We've explored the need for you to have a knowledge of the history of your home in order to take measured steps in any efforts to see it change. We've addressed the damage that transience does to society in general and ministry in particular, demanding that Christians embody a theology of place and a clear sense of sentness. In the end, we encountered the new humanity that awaits us in full when God comes to claim the earth, but which must be fought for now, in earnest, if we are to be biblically faithful or expect to see a catalytic change. And if you are the leader I believe you to be, then your first response will be to take what you've gained and *do* something.

the right words + the right time = CHANGE

That is our equation, and *time* is of great import. You need time. Time to sit with these ideas. Time to engage your friends and family. Time to engage those you lead or those who are leading you. You need time to work through the questions I've asked and to work through those that the Spirit has surfaced in your heart. You need time to simply be present, in your place, with these ideas. And then, armed with the right words and seasoned with enough time, go boldly, and don't stop until the good Lord says so.

Epilogue

Fury in Evening Land

If we lift our hands in orchestrated ecstasy
to the God we cannot see but refuse to raise
our voices in solidarity with brothers and sisters
who grieve before our very eyes then we are
indeed fully opiated addicts to religion's needle,
and whatever flimflam of hope that is within us
is gelded and knows nothing of the fury of love.

—John Blase, *The Beautiful Due* blog

FERGUSON AND BEYOND

As this manuscript goes to print, there have unfortunately been continued injustices in such places as Ferguson, Missouri. One of the most recent incidents being the murder in June 2015 of nine black people by a lone white gunman on a Wednesday night in the historic Emanuel African Methodist Episcopal Church in downtown Charleston, South Carolina. To say that this is a reality in our country that needs renovation is an understatement. I stand by the thoughts presented below; they originally appeared on my blog. In August 2014, Ed Stetzer invited me to share them on his blog, *The Exchange*.

It's Time to Listen

On Saturday, August 9, 2014, Michael Brown, an unarmed black teenager, was shot and killed by Darren Wilson, a police officer, in Ferguson, Missouri, a suburb of St. Louis. The killing ignited more than a week of protest and drew outrage on social media outlets like Twitter and Facebook. I want to believe with all that is in me that had a Jesus-centered, socially conscious, transcultural community been in place in Ferguson, this tragedy would not have happened. I realize I cannot say that with complete certainty, for in many ways, *anything* can happen. But the absence of such a community left Ferguson, both the place and the people, vulnerable to being mistreated. Of this I am resolute.

I say that in one breath, and with the next I know for certain that there are those working in Ferguson for the common good. They were there long before Michael Brown was slain. And by all accounts, they will be there long after. They may not make the evening news, but they are there, working for what former Ferguson resident Rev. Traci D. Blackmon calls...

a Ferguson that can be. A Ferguson absent of racial
profiling, a Ferguson in which all of the children
receive a quality education from accredited school
systems, a Ferguson where families are not economically imprisoned by joblessness and predatory traffic
courts, a Ferguson where all children feel safe and
protected in their neighborhoods, a morally just
Ferguson.[23]

Working Toward Whiteness

"I'm sorry for being white!" His comment glowed from the
computer screen with such weight that for a moment it was as
if it was etched there permanently. What, you may wonder, was
the context of this comment? It was written on the Facebook
wall of one of my congregants. It was written by her father in
response to her trying to explain why Ferguson has been so
painful for so many in the African American community. I was
truly in disbelief. He was once a Southern Baptist pastor.

What I wanted to write back but didn't is, "Are you?" Are
you sorry for being white? Or are you sick of having the privilege of your whiteness surfaced and challenged by the plight of
my (our) collective "blackness"? Are you tired of "us" pointing
out the obvious inequalities of our society? Should I, as a Cre-
ole, mixed-race, African American evangelical leader sit quietly
by, not saying a word about what has transpired in Ferguson
and many other cities, so that your white daughter would not

feel compelled to speak out and the comfort of your reality would remain?

This comment is filled with the type of sarcastic, defensive vitriol that has populated the Twitter time lines, Instagram feeds, and Facebook posts of so many white evangelicals. And it seems to capture the mind-set of the majority. Note, I said majority, not all. I make that point to ensure that I (with my white wife, tri-racial children, and transcultural church) won't be labeled here, as I have been in other places, a "racist," "race-baiter," or "divisive."

This comment captures the very reason why many African Americans feel so alone in this, and why men like my friend and mentor Pastor Thabiti Anyabwile have had to call out our camp for being saved but silent. This comment, and others that seem to quickly jump to the defense of Officer Wilson with disregard for the fact that a human life has been taken, creates a struggle in me that I must diligently work against: the belief that my white brothers and sisters simply don't care about the African American narrative in this country or that they don't believe it has enough value to be acknowledged.

The African American Narrative: A Series of "Justified" and "Routine" Stops

I am six foot five. I weigh two hundred seventy pounds. I've been called imposing. The police have stopped me, both walking and driving, nearly once a year since I was fifteen years old. Though I have been asked to leave my vehicle, thrown to the ground and against my vehicle, interrogated, frisked, and cuffed on these occasions, I've not been cited. Not once.

Until you feel the humiliation of this moment, particularly as a "decent, civilized, educated black"—yes, that's an actual quote of how someone referred to me once, behind my back of course—you cannot say that it is an anomaly. You cannot say that someone was just doing his or her job.

The most troubling of these incidents took place just a few years ago in Texas. Breanna and I were driving to my childhood home of Louisiana. We were pulled over, but I wasn't speeding. I wasn't driving erratically. I wasn't intoxicated. And it was broad daylight.

Two officers approached our vehicle, and when the lead saw me, he immediately placed his hand on his firearm. Breanna was visibly nervous. We'd just been joking sarcastically about hoping we didn't get pulled over in Texas for being an interracial couple. Then, in a flash, the joke became reality.

The officer asked me to step out of my vehicle. I refused. By this time I'd earned a master's in criminal justice. My focus in this degree was case law and judiciary process, which of course included an extensive study of policing histories and practices. So yes, I refused to get out of the car. But my wife pleaded and the officer demanded, so I complied.

The officer immediately grabbed me and began asking me where I was coming from, where I was going, and if I had anything in my vehicle of "concern." Meanwhile, the other officer interrogated my wife and asked if she was being held against her will. Really? Riding in the front seat, with a tri-racial child in the back? The lead officer, hand still on his firearm, began to try to frisk me. Again, I refused. The law says I *should* comply (*Pennsylvania v. Mimms*) and step out of the vehicle. But the law does not allow for illegal search of my person or property. I stated this to him. He became enraged, breathing threats and calling me "boy." It took the other officer to calm him down. Finally, with a lack of any justifiable reason to hold us, they let us go. I've never been so angry. Breanna never felt so humiliated.

These experiences are not mere anecdote. This is systemic.

A System of Injustice

Regarding the events in Ferguson, many have asked me, "Where's the injustice here? Where's the injustice in this case?" They follow it with requests for proof: "Has there been an unbiased account of what actually happened?" Or they angrily rebuke, "You really should wait for all of the facts before you speak on this!"

They have missed the forest for the trees.

I recently recommended the book *Working Toward Whiteness: How America's Immigrants Became White* by David R. Roediger to an Italian pastor friend in LA. After reading the first ten pages, my pastor friend sent this to me:

So for fear of losing control and being tainted by the
culture of the immigrant, Anglo-Europeans set up

systems of segregation and oppression to protect their
own cultural heritage, resulting in the oppression
of both immigrants and minority cultures. [These
systems included] housing and labor, where conforming brought reward and not conforming resulted in
oppression, hence the injustices dealt upon the ethnic
minorities, even today? Am I reading this correctly?

Yes! A resounding yes! He was made alive with truth. You
see, this issue is bigger than Michael Brown. It's bigger even
than recently deceased (at the hands of two officers), report-
edly mentally challenged Kajieme Powell. For these situations
merely serve to shine a light, not only on the systemic inequalities that African Americans are and have been subject to, but
also on what is actually in the hearts of many white Americans,
even those who claim to profess Christ as Savior, Lord, and
example.

We live in an oppressive system, strategically engineered to
subvert the progress of entire people groups and benefit the
progress of another. This is the injustice.

We are still reeling from the effects of slavery, Jim Crow,
redlining, and all associated behaviors. And before the phrase
"Get over it. It's in the past" begins to form on your lips, consider
my position. Consider that every time I look into my father's
eyes and see the pale blue rim around them, set back in his very
dark skin, or when I look at the texture of my mother's nearly

porcelain skin tone, I still see the residue of what I'm supposed to get over.

It is these injustices that will not allow white evangelicals to admit they have built their lives on the backs of the oppressive systems their grandfathers constructed.

It is these injustices that would lend their opinion immediately in favor of the officer and against the men whose lives were taken by them.

It is these injustices that would legitimize the death of a teenager by calling him a thug, thief, and an aggressor. It is these injustices that would legitimize the death of Kajieme Powell outside of St. Louis, another twenty-five-year-old mentally challenged man blocks from his home in Los Angeles, a new father holding a BB gun in the toy section of Walmart, and a father of six in New York.[24]

Since these victims, like most from where they sprang, are "this way," apparently they "deserve to die." Since the justice system is not perfect but fair toward all people, this is apparently the outcome of "their choices." These sentiments are sickening (and actual quotes, by the way). These sentiments seem to be carried by many in majority culture. It lacks any aroma of the gospel. It lacks any essence of the great grace of Christ, upon which we say our faith is built.

A Comfortable Division

I am nearly positive that this article will divide, and in that I am perfectly comfortable. My minority brothers and sisters, in almost melodic unison, will read this and feel heard, valued, and appreciated. They will feel as if they can breathe again.

While from what I see in social media and from a history of being willing to wrestle with these things among people in the majority culture, there will be a resounding cacophony of either silence or rebuke, ridicule, and complaint from others.

But where I am presently is where I was last Monday when I tweeted, "I have two daughters. I daily pray for a son. But if he'll be in danger for being black and large, perhaps I should stop praying." That is how I feel down to my soul. And disowning those feelings will not produce the "progress" my white evangelical friends say they want.

In an interview, Dr. King once said with respect to the civil rights movement:

> The most pervasive mistake I have made was in believing that because our cause was just, we could be sure that the white ministers of the South, once their Christian consciences were challenged, would rise to our aid. I felt that white ministers would take our cause to the white power structures. I ended up, of course, chastened and disillusioned.[25]

I am praying that *here, now,* this mistake will be rectified. I want to believe that you *will* rise to our aid, and that you would agree that a silent Christian who avoids applying the gospel to issues of injustice—though those issues may be uneasy, unclear, or politicized—upholds the very structures that purport and perpetuate injustice.

> A true and appropriate answer to our race problem,
> as to many others, would be a restoration of our com-
> munities—it being understood that a community,
> properly speaking, cannot exclude or mistreat any of
> its members.
> —Wendell Berry, *The Hidden Wound*

Notes

1. Richard Florida, *Who's Your City? How the Creative Economy Is Making Where to Live the Most Important Decision of Your Life* (New York: Basic Books, 2008), 8–9.

2. Florida, *Who's Your City?*, 4–5.

3. Martin Luther King Jr., *Why We Can't Wait* (Boston: Beacon, 1986), 86–87.

4. Quoted in Frederick Allen, *Atlanta Rising: The Invention of an International City 1946–1996* (Marietta, GA: Longstreet, 1996), vii.

5. Al Wolters, "Worldview and Textual Criticism in 2 Peter 3:10," *Westminster Theological Journal* 49 (1987): 405–13, www.allofliferedeemed.co.uk/Wolters/AMW 2Peter3.pdf.

6. Albert E. Brumley, "This World Is Not My Home," © 1965 Albert E. Brumley and Sons.

7. Isaac Watts, *The Psalms of David, Imitated in the Language of the New Testament, and Adapted to the Christian Use and Worship* (Albany, NY: Websters & Skinners, and Daniel Steele, 1817), 218.

8. Barry Holstun Lopez, *About This Life: Journeys on the Threshold of Memory* (New York: Vintage, 1998), 132.

9. Frederick Allen, *Atlanta Rising,* 145.

10. Allen, *Atlanta Rising,* 39–40.

11. Allen, *Atlanta Rising,* 180.

12. Allen, *Atlanta Rising,* 144.

13. Allen, *Atlanta Rising,* 200.

14. Larry Keating, *Atlanta: Race, Class, and Urban Expansion* (Philadelphia: Temple University Press, 2001), 20.

15. David Harvey, "From Space to Place and Back Again: Reflections on the Condition of Postmodernity," in *Mapping the Futures: Local Cultures, Global Change*, ed. Jon Bird et al. (London: Routledge, 1993), chap. 1.

16. Yi-Fu Tuan, *Space and Place: The Perspective of Experience* (Minneapolis: University of Minnesota Press, 1977), 199.

17. Albert M. Wolters, *Creation Regained: Biblical Basics for a Reformational Worldview* (Grand Rapids: Eerdmans, 1985), 57–58, 61.

18. Sally Lloyd-Jones, *The Jesus Storybook Bible: Every Story Whispers His Name* (Grand Rapids: Zonderkidz, 2007), 149.

19. Timothy Keller, "What Is (Christian) Cultural Renewal? (Part 1)," leadership training lecture, Redeemer Presbyterian Church, New York, May 5, 2003, http://sermons2 .redeemer.com/sermons/what-christian-cultural-renewal -part-1.

20. Mark A. Noll, *The Scandal of the Evangelical Mind* (Grand Rapids: Eerdmans, 1994), 51.

21. Quoted in Chris Hamnett, *Unequal City: London in the Global Arena* (London: Routledge, 2003), 146–7.

22. John Saillant, *Black Puritan, Black Republican: The Life and Thought of Lemuel Haynes, 1753–1833* (New York: Oxford University Press, 2003), 32.

23. Rev. Traci D. Blackmon, "Reflections on Ferguson: 3 Distinct Perspectives," *St. Louis Post-Dispatch,* October 4, 2014, www.stltoday.com/news/local/metro/reflections -on-ferguson-distinct-perspectives/collection_1489a 313-61e4-5d5b-a333-c63d618ea8c4.html.

24. Jesse Singal, "Kajieme Powell Died Because Police Have Become America's Mental-Health Workers," *New York,* August 22, 2014, http://nymag.com/scienceofus/2014/08 /police-kajieme-powell-and-mental-illness.html#. And Breanna Edwards, "4 Dead Unarmed Men and the Police: What You Need to Know," *The Root,* August 15, 2014, www.theroot.com/articles/culture/2014/08/_4_dead _unarmed_men_and_the_police_what_you_need_to _know.html.

25. Martin Luther King Jr., interview by Alex Haley, *Playboy,* January 1965, www.alex-haley.com/alex_haley_martin _luther_king_interview.htm.